50 Asian Cuisine Recipes for Home

By: Kelly Johnson

Table of Contents

- Pad Thai
- Sushi Rolls
- Chicken Teriyaki
- Beef and Broccoli Stir Fry
- Miso Soup
- Kimchi Fried Rice
- Thai Green Curry
- Ramen Noodles
- Shrimp Tempura
- Pork Dumplings
- General Tso's Chicken
- Bibimbap
- Vietnamese Pho
- Coconut Curry Chicken
- Japanese Curry Rice
- Spring Rolls
- Teriyaki Salmon
- Fried Rice
- Mapo Tofu
- Beef Bulgogi
- Chicken Katsu
- Thai Basil Chicken
- Steamed Dumplings
- Korean BBQ Ribs
- Vegetable Tempura
- Tom Yum Soup
- Yakisoba
- Szechuan Beef
- Peking Duck
- Gyoza
- Thai Red Curry
- Japanese Fried Chicken (Karaage)
- Pad See Ew
- Okonomiyaki
- Sweet and Sour Chicken

- Vietnamese Spring Rolls
- Bibim Guksu
- Chicken Satay
- Tom Kha Gai
- Teriyaki Tofu
- Chicken Yakitori
- Thai Peanut Noodles
- Korean Japchae
- Ramen Burger
- Stir-Fried Noodles
- Malaysian Laksa
- Korean Kimchi
- Singaporean Chili Crab
- Japanese Tempura
- Thai Mango Sticky Rice

Pad Thai

Ingredients:

- 8 oz (about 225g) flat rice noodles
- 2 tablespoons vegetable oil
- 2 cloves garlic, minced
- 1 small shallot, finely chopped
- 2 eggs, lightly beaten
- 8 oz (about 225g) protein of your choice (tofu, chicken, shrimp, or a combination)
- 2 cups bean sprouts
- 3 green onions, chopped
- 1/4 cup chopped peanuts
- Lime wedges, for serving
- Chopped cilantro, for garnish

For the sauce:

- 3 tablespoons tamarind paste
- 3 tablespoons fish sauce
- 2 tablespoons palm sugar or brown sugar
- 1 tablespoon soy sauce
- 1 tablespoon rice vinegar
- 1 teaspoon chili flakes (adjust to taste)

Instructions:

1. Prepare the noodles according to package instructions until they are just tender. Drain and rinse with cold water to stop the cooking process. Set aside.
2. In a small bowl, whisk together all the ingredients for the sauce until the sugar has dissolved. Set aside.
3. Heat 1 tablespoon of oil in a large skillet or wok over medium-high heat. Add the garlic and shallot, and cook until fragrant, about 1 minute.
4. Push the garlic and shallot to one side of the pan and add the beaten eggs to the other side. Scramble the eggs until cooked through, then mix them with the garlic and shallot.

5. Add the remaining tablespoon of oil to the skillet, then add the protein of your choice (tofu, chicken, shrimp, or a combination). Cook until the protein is fully cooked and lightly browned.
6. Add the cooked noodles to the skillet, followed by the sauce. Toss everything together until well combined and heated through.
7. Add the bean sprouts and chopped green onions to the skillet, and toss until they are just wilted.
8. Remove the skillet from heat and sprinkle with chopped peanuts.
9. Serve the Pad Thai hot, garnished with lime wedges and chopped cilantro.

Enjoy your homemade Pad Thai! Adjust the ingredients and seasoning according to your taste preferences.

Sushi Rolls

Ingredients:

- 2 cups sushi rice
- 2 1/2 cups water
- 1/2 cup rice vinegar
- 1/4 cup sugar
- 1 teaspoon salt
- Nori (seaweed) sheets
- Assorted fillings (such as cucumber, avocado, carrots, crab sticks, cooked shrimp, or smoked salmon)
- Soy sauce, for dipping
- Pickled ginger and wasabi, for serving (optional)

Instructions:

1. Rinse the sushi rice under cold water until the water runs clear. Drain the rice well.
2. In a rice cooker or saucepan, combine the rinsed rice and water. Cook the rice according to the package instructions.
3. While the rice is cooking, prepare the sushi vinegar by combining the rice vinegar, sugar, and salt in a small saucepan. Heat over low heat until the sugar and salt are dissolved. Remove from heat and let it cool.
4. When the rice is cooked, transfer it to a large bowl and gently fold in the sushi vinegar until well combined. Be careful not to smash the rice grains.
5. Lay a sheet of nori on a bamboo sushi mat or a clean kitchen towel. With wet hands, spread a thin layer of sushi rice over the nori, leaving about 1 inch of the nori sheet uncovered at the top edge.
6. Arrange your desired fillings in a line across the center of the rice.
7. Using the bamboo mat or towel, roll the sushi tightly away from you, pressing gently as you roll to seal the ingredients inside. Moisten the uncovered edge of the nori with a little water to seal the roll.
8. Repeat the process with the remaining nori sheets and fillings.
9. Once all the rolls are assembled, use a sharp knife to slice each roll into bite-sized pieces.

10. Serve the sushi rolls with soy sauce for dipping. You can also serve them with pickled ginger and wasabi on the side, if desired.

Enjoy your homemade sushi rolls! Feel free to get creative with different fillings and variations.

Chicken Teriyaki

Ingredients:

- 4 boneless, skinless chicken breasts
- 1/2 cup soy sauce
- 1/4 cup mirin (Japanese sweet rice wine)
- 1/4 cup sake (Japanese rice wine) or dry sherry
- 2 tablespoons brown sugar
- 2 cloves garlic, minced
- 1 teaspoon grated ginger
- 1 tablespoon vegetable oil
- Sesame seeds and chopped green onions for garnish (optional)

Instructions:

1. In a bowl, whisk together the soy sauce, mirin, sake, brown sugar, garlic, and ginger to make the teriyaki sauce. Set aside.
2. Place the chicken breasts between two pieces of plastic wrap and pound them to an even thickness, about 1/2 inch thick.
3. Heat the vegetable oil in a large skillet over medium-high heat. Add the chicken breasts and cook until golden brown on both sides, about 4-5 minutes per side.
4. Pour the teriyaki sauce over the chicken breasts in the skillet. Reduce the heat to medium-low and simmer for 6-8 minutes, or until the chicken is cooked through and the sauce has thickened slightly.
5. Remove the chicken from the skillet and let it rest for a few minutes before slicing it into strips.
6. Serve the sliced chicken teriyaki over rice or noodles, drizzled with the sauce from the skillet. Garnish with sesame seeds and chopped green onions, if desired.
7. Enjoy your homemade Chicken Teriyaki!

Feel free to adjust the ingredients and seasoning according to your taste preferences.

You can also add vegetables like broccoli, bell peppers, or carrots to the skillet along with the chicken for a more balanced meal.

Beef and Broccoli Stir Fry

Ingredients:

- 1 lb (450g) flank steak or sirloin, thinly sliced against the grain
- 1/4 cup soy sauce
- 2 tablespoons oyster sauce
- 1 tablespoon hoisin sauce
- 2 tablespoons brown sugar
- 2 cloves garlic, minced
- 1 teaspoon grated ginger
- 1 tablespoon cornstarch
- 2 tablespoons vegetable oil, divided
- 2 cups broccoli florets
- 1 small onion, thinly sliced
- Cooked rice, for serving
- Sesame seeds and sliced green onions for garnish (optional)

Instructions:

1. In a bowl, whisk together the soy sauce, oyster sauce, hoisin sauce, brown sugar, garlic, ginger, and cornstarch to make the sauce. Set aside.
2. Heat 1 tablespoon of vegetable oil in a large skillet or wok over high heat. Add the sliced beef and stir-fry for 2-3 minutes, or until browned. Remove the beef from the skillet and set aside.
3. In the same skillet, add the remaining tablespoon of vegetable oil. Add the broccoli florets and sliced onion, and stir-fry for 2-3 minutes, or until the vegetables are tender-crisp.
4. Return the cooked beef to the skillet. Pour the sauce over the beef and broccoli, and stir to coat everything evenly. Cook for an additional 1-2 minutes, or until the sauce has thickened slightly.
5. Remove the skillet from heat. Serve the beef and broccoli stir-fry hot over cooked rice. Garnish with sesame seeds and sliced green onions, if desired.
6. Enjoy your homemade Beef and Broccoli Stir Fry!

Feel free to customize this recipe by adding other vegetables such as bell peppers, mushrooms, or snap peas. You can also adjust the seasoning and sauce according to your taste preferences.

Miso Soup

Ingredients:

- 4 cups water or dashi (Japanese soup stock)
- 1/4 cup miso paste (white or red, depending on preference)
- 1/2 block tofu, cut into small cubes
- 2 green onions, thinly sliced
- 1 sheet nori (seaweed), cut into small strips (optional)
- 1 tablespoon soy sauce (optional)
- 1 teaspoon sesame oil (optional)

Instructions:

1. In a medium-sized pot, bring the water or dashi to a gentle boil over medium heat.
2. Once the water is boiling, add the tofu cubes to the pot. Let them cook for about 2-3 minutes, or until they are heated through.
3. Reduce the heat to low. In a small bowl, mix the miso paste with a ladleful of the hot water from the pot until it forms a smooth paste.
4. Slowly pour the miso paste mixture into the pot while stirring gently to incorporate it into the soup.
5. Add the sliced green onions to the soup. If desired, you can also add the nori strips, soy sauce, and sesame oil for extra flavor.
6. Let the soup simmer gently for another 1-2 minutes, making sure not to let it come to a boil again.
7. Taste the soup and adjust the seasoning if necessary, adding more miso paste, soy sauce, or sesame oil to taste.
8. Once the soup is heated through and the flavors have melded together, remove the pot from the heat.
9. Serve the miso soup hot in individual bowls, garnished with additional sliced green onions or nori strips if desired.
10. Enjoy your homemade Miso Soup!

Feel free to customize this recipe by adding other ingredients such as mushrooms, spinach, or seaweed. Adjust the proportions of miso paste and water/dashi according to your taste preferences for a stronger or milder miso flavor.

Kimchi Fried Rice

Ingredients:

- 2 cups cooked rice (preferably day-old rice)
- 1 cup kimchi, chopped
- 2 tablespoons kimchi juice (from the jar)
- 2 tablespoons vegetable oil
- 2 cloves garlic, minced
- 1 small onion, finely chopped
- 1 carrot, diced
- 1 cup cooked protein of your choice (such as diced chicken, pork, or tofu)
- 2 tablespoons soy sauce
- 1 tablespoon sesame oil
- 2 green onions, thinly sliced
- Toasted sesame seeds, for garnish (optional)
- Fried eggs, for serving (optional)

Instructions:

1. Heat the vegetable oil in a large skillet or wok over medium-high heat. Add the minced garlic and chopped onion, and cook until softened and fragrant, about 2-3 minutes.
2. Add the diced carrot to the skillet and cook for another 2-3 minutes, or until the carrot starts to soften.
3. Add the chopped kimchi to the skillet along with the kimchi juice, and stir-fry for 2-3 minutes to heat through and allow the flavors to meld.
4. Add the cooked rice to the skillet, breaking up any clumps with a spoon or spatula. Stir-fry the rice with the kimchi mixture until well combined.
5. Add the cooked protein of your choice (such as diced chicken, pork, or tofu) to the skillet, and stir-fry for another 2-3 minutes, or until heated through.
6. Drizzle the soy sauce and sesame oil over the fried rice, and toss everything together until evenly coated.
7. Cook for another 2-3 minutes, or until the fried rice is heated through and slightly crispy.
8. Remove the skillet from heat and stir in the sliced green onions.

9. Transfer the kimchi fried rice to serving plates or bowls. Garnish with toasted sesame seeds, if desired.
10. Serve the kimchi fried rice hot, optionally topped with a fried egg.

Enjoy your homemade Kimchi Fried Rice! Adjust the seasoning and ingredients according to your taste preferences.

Thai Green Curry

Ingredients:

- 2 tablespoons green curry paste
- 1 can (14 oz) coconut milk
- 1 cup chicken or vegetable broth
- 1 tablespoon vegetable oil
- 1 lb (450g) boneless chicken breast or thighs, thinly sliced (or substitute tofu or shrimp)
- 1 bell pepper, sliced
- 1 small eggplant, diced
- 1 cup sliced mushrooms
- 1 tablespoon fish sauce (or soy sauce for vegetarian/vegan option)
- 1 tablespoon brown sugar
- 1 cup Thai basil leaves (or regular basil leaves)
- Lime wedges, for serving
- Cooked rice, for serving

Instructions:

1. Heat the vegetable oil in a large skillet or pot over medium heat. Add the green curry paste and cook, stirring constantly, for 1-2 minutes until fragrant.
2. Pour in the coconut milk and chicken or vegetable broth. Stir well to combine and bring to a gentle simmer.
3. Add the sliced chicken (or tofu or shrimp) to the skillet and cook for 5-7 minutes, or until the chicken is cooked through.
4. Add the sliced bell pepper, diced eggplant, and sliced mushrooms to the skillet. Simmer for another 5-7 minutes, or until the vegetables are tender.
5. Stir in the fish sauce (or soy sauce) and brown sugar. Taste and adjust the seasoning as needed.
6. Remove the skillet from heat and stir in the Thai basil leaves until wilted.
7. Serve the Thai green curry hot over cooked rice. Garnish with lime wedges.
8. Enjoy your homemade Thai Green Curry!

Feel free to customize this recipe by adding other vegetables such as bamboo shoots, snow peas, or baby corn. Adjust the amount of green curry paste according to your desired level of spiciness.

Ramen Noodles

Ingredients:

- 4 cups chicken or vegetable broth
- 2 cups water
- 2 packs of instant ramen noodles (discard the seasoning packets or save them for another use)
- 2 boiled eggs, halved
- 2 cups sliced cooked chicken, pork, tofu, or shrimp
- 2 cups mixed vegetables (such as sliced mushrooms, spinach, bok choy, shredded carrots, or bean sprouts)
- 2 tablespoons soy sauce
- 1 tablespoon miso paste (optional)
- 1 tablespoon sesame oil
- 2 green onions, thinly sliced
- 1 sheet nori (seaweed), sliced (optional)
- Chili oil or Sriracha sauce, for serving (optional)

Instructions:

1. In a large pot, bring the chicken or vegetable broth and water to a boil over medium-high heat.
2. Add the ramen noodles to the pot and cook according to the package instructions, usually about 3-4 minutes.
3. While the noodles are cooking, prepare your toppings. Boil the eggs, slice the cooked chicken or pork, and prepare the vegetables.
4. Once the noodles are cooked, reduce the heat to low. Add the soy sauce, miso paste (if using), and sesame oil to the pot. Stir to combine.
5. Divide the cooked noodles among serving bowls. Arrange the boiled egg halves, sliced cooked protein, and mixed vegetables on top of the noodles.
6. Ladle the hot broth over the noodles and toppings in each bowl.
7. Garnish each bowl with sliced green onions and nori strips, if desired.
8. Serve the ramen noodles hot, with chili oil or Sriracha sauce on the side for extra heat if desired.
9. Enjoy your homemade Ramen Noodles!

Feel free to customize your ramen noodles by adding other toppings such as sliced bamboo shoots, corn kernels, or narutomaki (fish cake). Adjust the seasoning to taste with soy sauce, miso paste, or other flavorings.

Shrimp Tempura

Ingredients:

- 12 large shrimp, peeled and deveined, tails left on
- 1 cup all-purpose flour
- 1/2 cup cornstarch
- 1 teaspoon baking powder
- 1 cup ice-cold water
- Vegetable oil, for frying
- Tempura dipping sauce (recipe below)
- Optional: Tempura dipping sauce (recipe below), grated daikon radish, grated ginger, or sliced green onions for serving

Instructions:

1. Prepare the tempura dipping sauce (recipe below) and set aside.
2. In a large bowl, whisk together the all-purpose flour, cornstarch, and baking powder.
3. Gradually pour in the ice-cold water while stirring, just until the batter is combined. Be careful not to overmix; it's okay if there are a few lumps.
4. Heat the vegetable oil in a deep fryer or large pot to 350°F (180°C).
5. Pat the shrimp dry with paper towels. Dredge each shrimp in the batter, shaking off any excess.
6. Carefully lower the battered shrimp into the hot oil, a few at a time, and fry for 2-3 minutes, or until golden brown and crispy.
7. Remove the shrimp from the oil using a slotted spoon and transfer them to a plate lined with paper towels to drain.
8. Repeat the process with the remaining shrimp, ensuring not to overcrowd the fryer or pot.
9. Serve the shrimp tempura hot, accompanied by the tempura dipping sauce and any additional condiments you prefer.
10. Enjoy your homemade Shrimp Tempura!

Tempura Dipping Sauce:

Ingredients:

- 1/2 cup soy sauce
- 1/4 cup mirin (Japanese sweet rice wine)
- 1 tablespoon sugar
- 1 cup dashi (Japanese soup stock) or water

Instructions:

1. In a small saucepan, combine the soy sauce, mirin, sugar, and dashi or water.
2. Bring the mixture to a gentle simmer over medium heat, stirring until the sugar has dissolved.
3. Remove the saucepan from heat and let the tempura dipping sauce cool to room temperature before serving.
4. Serve the tempura dipping sauce alongside your Shrimp Tempura.

Enjoy your crispy and delicious Shrimp Tempura with this simple recipe!

Pork Dumplings

Ingredients:

For the filling:

- 1/2 lb ground pork
- 1 cup finely chopped cabbage
- 2 green onions, finely chopped
- 2 cloves garlic, minced
- 1 tablespoon grated ginger
- 1 tablespoon soy sauce
- 1 tablespoon sesame oil
- 1 teaspoon sugar
- 1/2 teaspoon salt
- 1/4 teaspoon black pepper
- 1 egg, lightly beaten
- 30-40 round dumpling wrappers

For dipping sauce (optional):

- 2 tablespoons soy sauce
- 1 tablespoon rice vinegar
- 1 teaspoon sesame oil
- 1 teaspoon finely chopped green onions

Instructions:

1. In a large mixing bowl, combine the ground pork, chopped cabbage, green onions, garlic, ginger, soy sauce, sesame oil, sugar, salt, pepper, and beaten egg. Mix until well combined.
2. To assemble the dumplings, place a small spoonful of the filling in the center of each dumpling wrapper. Wet the edges of the wrapper with water using your fingertip. Fold the wrapper in half to form a half-moon shape, pressing the edges firmly to seal. You can also crimp the edges to create a decorative pattern.

3. Repeat the process with the remaining filling and wrappers until all the dumplings are assembled.
4. To cook the dumplings, you can either boil, steam, or pan-fry them:
    - To boil: Bring a large pot of water to a boil. Carefully add the dumplings and cook for 4-5 minutes, or until they float to the surface and are cooked through.
    - To steam: Place the dumplings in a single layer in a steamer basket lined with parchment paper. Steam over simmering water for 8-10 minutes, or until cooked through.
    - To pan-fry: Heat a tablespoon of oil in a non-stick skillet over medium heat. Add the dumplings in a single layer and cook for 2-3 minutes, or until the bottoms are golden brown. Add 1/4 cup of water to the skillet and cover with a lid. Steam the dumplings for another 4-5 minutes, or until cooked through and the water has evaporated.
5. While the dumplings are cooking, prepare the dipping sauce by combining soy sauce, rice vinegar, sesame oil, and chopped green onions in a small bowl.
6. Serve the cooked dumplings hot with the dipping sauce on the side.

Enjoy your homemade Pork Dumplings! You can also customize the filling by adding ingredients like shrimp, mushrooms, or water chestnuts.

General Tso's Chicken

Ingredients:

For the chicken:

- 1 lb boneless, skinless chicken thighs or breasts, cut into bite-sized pieces
- 1/2 cup cornstarch
- 2 eggs, beaten
- Vegetable oil, for frying

For the sauce:

- 1/4 cup soy sauce
- 2 tablespoons hoisin sauce
- 2 tablespoons rice vinegar
- 2 tablespoons honey
- 1 tablespoon sesame oil
- 2 cloves garlic, minced
- 1 tablespoon minced ginger
- 1 tablespoon cornstarch mixed with 2 tablespoons water (cornstarch slurry)
- Red pepper flakes or Sriracha sauce, to taste (optional)

For garnish:

- Sliced green onions
- Toasted sesame seeds
- Cooked rice, for serving

Instructions:

1. In a shallow dish, coat the chicken pieces evenly with cornstarch, shaking off any excess. Dip the cornstarch-coated chicken pieces into the beaten eggs, ensuring they are fully coated.

2. Heat vegetable oil in a large skillet or wok over medium-high heat. Once the oil is hot, add the chicken pieces in batches and fry until golden brown and crispy, about 3-4 minutes per side. Transfer the cooked chicken to a plate lined with paper towels to drain excess oil.
3. In a separate bowl, whisk together the soy sauce, hoisin sauce, rice vinegar, honey, sesame oil, minced garlic, and minced ginger to make the sauce.
4. Heat a tablespoon of vegetable oil in a large skillet or wok over medium heat. Add the minced garlic and ginger, and cook for 1-2 minutes until fragrant.
5. Pour the sauce mixture into the skillet and bring it to a simmer. Let it cook for 1-2 minutes until slightly thickened.
6. Stir in the cornstarch slurry and continue to cook for another 1-2 minutes, or until the sauce has thickened to your desired consistency. If you like your General Tso's Chicken spicy, add red pepper flakes or Sriracha sauce to taste.
7. Add the cooked chicken pieces to the skillet and toss until they are evenly coated with the sauce.
8. Remove the skillet from heat and garnish the General Tso's Chicken with sliced green onions and toasted sesame seeds.
9. Serve hot over cooked rice.

Enjoy your homemade General Tso's Chicken! Adjust the seasoning and spice level according to your taste preferences.

Bibimbap

Ingredients:

For the Bibimbap:

- 2 cups cooked short-grain rice
- 2 cups assorted vegetables (such as spinach, carrots, bean sprouts, mushrooms, zucchini, and bell peppers), julienned or sliced
- 1 cup protein of your choice (such as thinly sliced beef, tofu, or cooked shrimp)
- 4 eggs
- Vegetable oil, for cooking
- Sesame seeds, for garnish
- Thinly sliced green onions, for garnish

For the Bibimbap sauce:

- 4 tablespoons gochujang (Korean red pepper paste)
- 2 tablespoons soy sauce
- 1 tablespoon sesame oil
- 1 tablespoon rice vinegar
- 1 tablespoon honey or sugar
- 1 clove garlic, minced
- 1 teaspoon grated ginger

Instructions:

1. Cook the short-grain rice according to the package instructions. Once cooked, fluff the rice with a fork and set aside.
2. Prepare the Bibimbap sauce by whisking together the gochujang, soy sauce, sesame oil, rice vinegar, honey or sugar, minced garlic, and grated ginger in a small bowl. Set aside.
3. Cook each type of vegetable separately in boiling water until just tender, then drain and set aside. You can also sauté or stir-fry the vegetables in a little vegetable oil until cooked.
4. Cook the protein of your choice (such as thinly sliced beef, tofu, or cooked shrimp) in a skillet with a little vegetable oil until cooked through. Season with salt and pepper, if desired.

5. In a separate non-stick skillet, fry the eggs sunny-side-up or over-easy until the whites are set but the yolks are still runny.
6. To assemble the Bibimbap, divide the cooked rice among serving bowls. Arrange the cooked vegetables and protein on top of the rice, leaving space for the fried egg.
7. Place a fried egg on top of each bowl of Bibimbap.
8. Drizzle the Bibimbap sauce over the rice, vegetables, and protein.
9. Garnish the Bibimbap with sesame seeds and thinly sliced green onions.
10. Serve the Bibimbap immediately, with extra Bibimbap sauce on the side for those who want more spice.

Enjoy your homemade Bibimbap! Mix everything together before eating to combine all the flavors and textures. Feel free to customize the ingredients and adjust the spice level according to your taste preferences.

Vietnamese Pho

Ingredients:

For the broth:

- 2 onions, halved
- 1 piece (about 3 inches) fresh ginger, halved lengthwise
- 4-5 pounds beef bones (such as marrow bones and knuckle bones)
- 2 cinnamon sticks
- 3 star anise
- 4-5 cloves
- 1 cardamom pod
- 1 tablespoon coriander seeds
- 1 tablespoon salt
- 1 tablespoon sugar
- 1/4 cup fish sauce
- Water

For the soup:

- 1 pound dried rice noodles (banh pho)
- 1 pound beef sirloin, thinly sliced
- 1 onion, thinly sliced
- 4 green onions, thinly sliced
- 1/2 cup chopped fresh cilantro
- 1/2 cup chopped fresh mint
- 1/2 cup chopped fresh Thai basil
- Bean sprouts, for serving
- Lime wedges, for serving
- Sriracha sauce, for serving
- Hoisin sauce, for serving

Instructions:

1. To make the broth, char the halved onions and ginger over an open flame or under a broiler until lightly blackened. Rinse them under cold water and set aside.

2. In a large pot, add the beef bones and cover with cold water. Bring to a boil over high heat and let it boil vigorously for 10-15 minutes. This will help to remove any impurities.
3. Drain the bones and rinse them under cold water. Clean the pot and return the bones to it.
4. Add the charred onions and ginger, cinnamon sticks, star anise, cloves, cardamom pod, coriander seeds, salt, sugar, and fish sauce to the pot. Cover with cold water.
5. Bring the pot to a simmer over medium-low heat. Skim off any foam or impurities that rise to the surface.
6. Simmer the broth gently for at least 3-4 hours, preferably longer, up to 6-8 hours, to develop the flavors. Add more water as needed to keep the bones submerged.
7. Strain the broth through a fine-mesh strainer or cheesecloth into a clean pot. Discard the solids. Taste the broth and adjust the seasoning if needed, adding more salt, sugar, or fish sauce to taste.
8. Prepare the rice noodles according to the package instructions. Drain and rinse them under cold water.
9. Divide the cooked rice noodles among serving bowls. Top with thinly sliced beef sirloin and onion slices.
10. Ladle the hot broth over the noodles and beef. The hot broth will cook the beef slices.
11. Serve the Pho hot, garnished with sliced green onions, chopped cilantro, mint, Thai basil, and bean sprouts. Serve lime wedges, Sriracha sauce, and hoisin sauce on the side for each diner to customize their soup.
12. Enjoy your homemade Vietnamese Pho!

Feel free to customize your Pho with additional toppings such as sliced jalapeños, Thai bird's eye chilies, or sliced cooked beef tendon. Adjust the seasoning and spice level according to your taste preferences.

Coconut Curry Chicken

Ingredients:

- 1.5 lbs boneless, skinless chicken breasts or thighs, cut into bite-sized pieces
- 2 tablespoons vegetable oil
- 1 onion, finely chopped
- 3 cloves garlic, minced
- 1 tablespoon grated ginger
- 2 tablespoons curry powder
- 1 teaspoon ground turmeric
- 1 teaspoon ground coriander
- 1/2 teaspoon ground cumin
- 1/2 teaspoon chili powder (adjust to taste)
- 1 can (14 oz) coconut milk
- 1 cup chicken broth
- 2 tablespoons fish sauce (or soy sauce for a vegetarian version)
- 2 tablespoons brown sugar
- Juice of 1 lime
- Salt and pepper, to taste
- Fresh cilantro, chopped, for garnish
- Cooked rice, for serving

Instructions:

1. Heat the vegetable oil in a large skillet or pot over medium heat. Add the chopped onion and cook until softened, about 3-4 minutes.
2. Add the minced garlic and grated ginger to the skillet, and cook for an additional 1-2 minutes until fragrant.
3. Stir in the curry powder, ground turmeric, ground coriander, ground cumin, and chili powder. Cook the spices for about 1 minute until they are fragrant and toasted.
4. Add the bite-sized chicken pieces to the skillet, and cook until they are lightly browned on all sides, about 5-6 minutes.
5. Pour in the coconut milk and chicken broth, and stir to combine. Bring the mixture to a simmer, then reduce the heat to low and let it simmer gently for 15-20 minutes, or until the chicken is cooked through and tender.

6. Stir in the fish sauce (or soy sauce), brown sugar, and lime juice. Season with salt and pepper, to taste. Adjust the seasoning and sweetness according to your taste preferences.
7. Serve the Coconut Curry Chicken hot over cooked rice. Garnish with chopped fresh cilantro.
8. Enjoy your homemade Coconut Curry Chicken!

Feel free to customize this recipe by adding your favorite vegetables such as bell peppers, carrots, or potatoes. You can also adjust the spiciness by adding more or less chili powder, or by adding chopped fresh chili peppers.

Japanese Curry Rice

Ingredients:

For the curry sauce:

- 2 tablespoons vegetable oil
- 1 onion, finely chopped
- 2 carrots, peeled and diced
- 2 potatoes, peeled and diced
- 2 cloves garlic, minced
- 1 tablespoon grated ginger
- 2 tablespoons curry powder
- 1 tablespoon garam masala (optional, for extra flavor)
- 3 cups chicken or vegetable broth
- 2 tablespoons soy sauce
- 2 tablespoons Worcestershire sauce
- 1 tablespoon honey or sugar
- Salt and pepper, to taste
- 2 tablespoons cornstarch mixed with 2 tablespoons water (cornstarch slurry)

For serving:

- Cooked white rice
- Pickled ginger (optional)
- Fukujinzuke (pickled radish) (optional)

Instructions:

1. Heat the vegetable oil in a large pot over medium heat. Add the chopped onion and cook until softened, about 3-4 minutes.
2. Add the diced carrots and potatoes to the pot, and cook for an additional 5 minutes, stirring occasionally.
3. Stir in the minced garlic and grated ginger, and cook for another 1-2 minutes until fragrant.

4. Add the curry powder and garam masala (if using) to the pot, and cook for 1 minute, stirring constantly to toast the spices.
5. Pour in the chicken or vegetable broth, soy sauce, Worcestershire sauce, and honey or sugar. Stir to combine.
6. Bring the mixture to a simmer, then reduce the heat to low and let it simmer gently for 15-20 minutes, or until the vegetables are tender.
7. Taste the curry sauce and adjust the seasoning with salt and pepper, if needed.
8. Stir in the cornstarch slurry, a little at a time, until the sauce thickens to your desired consistency. Cook for an additional 2-3 minutes to allow the sauce to thicken completely.
9. To serve, spoon the curry sauce over cooked white rice. Garnish with pickled ginger and fukujinzuke, if desired.
10. Enjoy your homemade Japanese Curry Rice!

Feel free to customize your Japanese Curry Rice by adding other ingredients such as sliced onions, bell peppers, or protein such as chicken, beef, or tofu. Adjust the spiciness level by adding more or less curry powder or garam masala.

Spring Rolls

Ingredients:

- 8-10 round rice paper wrappers
- 8-10 large shrimp, peeled, deveined, and cooked
- 1 cup vermicelli noodles, cooked according to package instructions
- 1 cup shredded lettuce
- 1 cup shredded carrots
- 1 cup cucumber, julienned
- Fresh herbs (such as mint, cilantro, and Thai basil)
- Hoisin sauce, for dipping
- Peanut sauce, for dipping (optional)

Instructions:

1. Prepare all the filling ingredients by cooking the vermicelli noodles according to the package instructions, cooking and cooling the shrimp, and prepping the vegetables.
2. Fill a shallow dish with warm water. Dip one rice paper wrapper into the water for a few seconds until it becomes pliable. Place the wet rice paper wrapper on a clean, damp kitchen towel or a plate.
3. Arrange a few shrimp halves (or whole shrimp), vermicelli noodles, shredded lettuce, carrots, cucumber, and fresh herbs in the center of the rice paper wrapper, leaving some space on the sides.
4. Fold the bottom edge of the rice paper wrapper over the filling, then fold in the sides, and roll it up tightly into a cylinder, similar to rolling a burrito.
5. Repeat the process with the remaining rice paper wrappers and filling ingredients.
6. Serve the spring rolls immediately with hoisin sauce or peanut sauce for dipping.
7. Enjoy your homemade Vietnamese Spring Rolls as an appetizer or light meal!

Feel free to customize your spring rolls by adding other ingredients such as cooked chicken, tofu, or avocado. You can also experiment with different dipping sauces or add a spicy kick with Sriracha or chili sauce.

Teriyaki Salmon

Ingredients:

- 4 salmon fillets (about 6 oz each), skin-on or skinless
- 1/4 cup soy sauce
- 2 tablespoons honey
- 2 tablespoons rice vinegar
- 2 cloves garlic, minced
- 1 tablespoon grated ginger
- 1 tablespoon sesame oil
- 1 tablespoon cornstarch
- 1 tablespoon water
- Optional garnish: sliced green onions and sesame seeds

Instructions:

1. In a small bowl, whisk together the soy sauce, honey, rice vinegar, minced garlic, grated ginger, and sesame oil to make the teriyaki sauce.
2. In a separate small bowl, mix the cornstarch and water to make a slurry.
3. Place the salmon fillets in a shallow dish or a resealable plastic bag. Pour half of the teriyaki sauce over the salmon, reserving the other half for later. Marinate the salmon in the refrigerator for at least 30 minutes, or up to 2 hours.
4. Preheat your grill to medium-high heat or preheat your oven to 400°F (200°C).
5. If using a grill, lightly oil the grill grates to prevent sticking. If baking, line a baking sheet with parchment paper or foil for easy cleanup.
6. Remove the salmon from the marinade and discard the marinade. Place the salmon fillets on the grill or on the prepared baking sheet.
7. Grill the salmon for 4-5 minutes per side, or until cooked through and flaky. If baking, bake the salmon in the preheated oven for 12-15 minutes, or until cooked through.
8. While the salmon is cooking, pour the reserved teriyaki sauce into a small saucepan. Bring the sauce to a simmer over medium heat.
9. Stir the cornstarch slurry again to ensure it is well combined, then slowly pour it into the simmering sauce while stirring constantly. Cook the sauce for 1-2 minutes, or until it thickens to your desired consistency.

10. Once the salmon is cooked through, remove it from the grill or oven. Drizzle the thickened teriyaki sauce over the salmon fillets.
11. Garnish the teriyaki salmon with sliced green onions and sesame seeds, if desired.
12. Serve the teriyaki salmon hot with your favorite side dishes, such as steamed rice and stir-fried vegetables.
13. Enjoy your homemade Teriyaki Salmon!

Feel free to adjust the sweetness or saltiness of the teriyaki sauce according to your taste preferences by adding more honey or soy sauce. You can also add a splash of mirin (Japanese sweet rice wine) for extra flavor.

Fried Rice

Ingredients:

- 3 cups cooked rice (preferably day-old rice)
- 2 tablespoons vegetable oil
- 2 eggs, beaten
- 1 cup mixed vegetables (such as peas, carrots, corn, and bell peppers)
- 2 cloves garlic, minced
- 2 green onions, thinly sliced
- 2 tablespoons soy sauce
- 1 tablespoon oyster sauce (optional)
- Salt and pepper, to taste
- Sesame oil, for drizzling (optional)
- Cooked protein of your choice (such as diced chicken, shrimp, or tofu), optional

Instructions:

1. If you don't have day-old rice, cook the rice according to package instructions and spread it out on a baking sheet to cool and dry slightly.
2. Heat 1 tablespoon of vegetable oil in a large skillet or wok over medium-high heat. Add the beaten eggs and scramble them until cooked through. Remove the scrambled eggs from the skillet and set aside.
3. In the same skillet, add the remaining tablespoon of vegetable oil. Add the minced garlic and cook for about 30 seconds until fragrant.
4. Add the mixed vegetables to the skillet and cook until they are tender, about 3-4 minutes.
5. Add the cooked rice to the skillet, breaking up any clumps with a spatula. Stir-fry the rice with the vegetables for 2-3 minutes until heated through.
6. Add the cooked protein (if using) to the skillet and stir to combine with the rice and vegetables.
7. Return the scrambled eggs to the skillet and stir to combine with the rice mixture.
8. Drizzle the soy sauce and oyster sauce (if using) over the rice mixture. Stir well to evenly distribute the sauces.
9. Add the sliced green onions to the skillet and toss everything together.
10. Season the fried rice with salt and pepper to taste. You can also drizzle a little sesame oil over the fried rice for extra flavor, if desired.

11. Cook for another 2-3 minutes, stirring occasionally, until everything is heated through and well combined.
12. Remove the skillet from heat and serve the fried rice hot.
13. Enjoy your homemade Fried Rice as a delicious and satisfying meal or side dish!

Feel free to customize your Fried Rice by adding other ingredients such as diced ham, cooked bacon, or chopped pineapple. You can also adjust the seasoning and sauce levels according to your taste preferences.

Mapo Tofu

Ingredients:

- 3 cups cooked rice (preferably day-old rice)
- 2 tablespoons vegetable oil
- 2 eggs, beaten
- 1 cup mixed vegetables (such as peas, carrots, corn, and bell peppers)
- 2 cloves garlic, minced
- 2 green onions, thinly sliced
- 2 tablespoons soy sauce
- 1 tablespoon oyster sauce (optional)
- Salt and pepper, to taste
- Sesame oil, for drizzling (optional)
- Cooked protein of your choice (such as diced chicken, shrimp, or tofu), optional

Instructions:

1. If you don't have day-old rice, cook the rice according to package instructions and spread it out on a baking sheet to cool and dry slightly.
2. Heat 1 tablespoon of vegetable oil in a large skillet or wok over medium-high heat. Add the beaten eggs and scramble them until cooked through. Remove the scrambled eggs from the skillet and set aside.
3. In the same skillet, add the remaining tablespoon of vegetable oil. Add the minced garlic and cook for about 30 seconds until fragrant.
4. Add the mixed vegetables to the skillet and cook until they are tender, about 3-4 minutes.
5. Add the cooked rice to the skillet, breaking up any clumps with a spatula. Stir-fry the rice with the vegetables for 2-3 minutes until heated through.
6. Add the cooked protein (if using) to the skillet and stir to combine with the rice and vegetables.
7. Return the scrambled eggs to the skillet and stir to combine with the rice mixture.
8. Drizzle the soy sauce and oyster sauce (if using) over the rice mixture. Stir well to evenly distribute the sauces.
9. Add the sliced green onions to the skillet and toss everything together.
10. Season the fried rice with salt and pepper to taste. You can also drizzle a little sesame oil over the fried rice for extra flavor, if desired.

11. Cook for another 2-3 minutes, stirring occasionally, until everything is heated through and well combined.
12. Remove the skillet from heat and serve the fried rice hot.
13. Enjoy your homemade Fried Rice as a delicious and satisfying meal or side dish!

Feel free to customize your Fried Rice by adding other ingredients such as diced ham, cooked bacon, or chopped pineapple. You can also adjust the seasoning and sauce levels according to your taste preferences.

Beef Bulgogi

Ingredients:

- 1 lb beef sirloin or ribeye, thinly sliced
- 1/4 cup soy sauce
- 2 tablespoons brown sugar
- 2 tablespoons sesame oil
- 3 cloves garlic, minced
- 1 tablespoon grated ginger
- 2 green onions, thinly sliced
- 1 tablespoon sesame seeds
- 1 tablespoon rice vinegar (optional, for extra tanginess)
- 1 tablespoon mirin or rice wine (optional, for sweetness)
- 1 tablespoon gochujang (Korean red pepper paste) (optional, for spiciness)
- 1/2 teaspoon black pepper
- 1 tablespoon vegetable oil, for cooking
- Optional garnish: sliced green onions and toasted sesame seeds

Instructions:

1. In a bowl, combine soy sauce, brown sugar, sesame oil, minced garlic, grated ginger, sliced green onions, sesame seeds, rice vinegar (if using), mirin or rice wine (if using), gochujang (if using), and black pepper. Stir until the sugar is dissolved and the marinade is well combined.
2. Add the thinly sliced beef to the marinade, making sure each piece is well coated. Cover the bowl with plastic wrap or transfer the beef and marinade to a resealable plastic bag. Marinate the beef in the refrigerator for at least 30 minutes, or up to 2 hours for best flavor.
3. Heat a tablespoon of vegetable oil in a large skillet or grill pan over medium-high heat.
4. Remove the marinated beef from the refrigerator and let it sit at room temperature for about 10 minutes.
5. Once the skillet or grill pan is hot, add the marinated beef slices in a single layer. Cook the beef in batches if necessary, to avoid overcrowding the pan.
6. Cook the beef slices for 2-3 minutes on each side, or until they are caramelized and cooked through.

7. Transfer the cooked beef bulgogi to a serving plate or bowl. Garnish with sliced green onions and toasted sesame seeds, if desired.
8. Serve the beef bulgogi hot with steamed rice and your favorite side dishes, such as kimchi and pickled vegetables.
9. Enjoy your homemade Beef Bulgogi as a flavorful and satisfying meal!

Feel free to adjust the marinade ingredients according to your taste preferences. You can also add thinly sliced vegetables such as onions, bell peppers, and mushrooms to the marinade or cook them alongside the beef for added flavor and texture.

Chicken Katsu

Ingredients:

- 1 lb beef sirloin or ribeye, thinly sliced
- 1/4 cup soy sauce
- 2 tablespoons brown sugar
- 2 tablespoons sesame oil
- 3 cloves garlic, minced
- 1 tablespoon grated ginger
- 2 green onions, thinly sliced
- 1 tablespoon sesame seeds
- 1 tablespoon rice vinegar (optional, for extra tanginess)
- 1 tablespoon mirin or rice wine (optional, for sweetness)
- 1 tablespoon gochujang (Korean red pepper paste) (optional, for spiciness)
- 1/2 teaspoon black pepper
- 1 tablespoon vegetable oil, for cooking
- Optional garnish: sliced green onions and toasted sesame seeds

Instructions:

1. In a bowl, combine soy sauce, brown sugar, sesame oil, minced garlic, grated ginger, sliced green onions, sesame seeds, rice vinegar (if using), mirin or rice wine (if using), gochujang (if using), and black pepper. Stir until the sugar is dissolved and the marinade is well combined.
2. Add the thinly sliced beef to the marinade, making sure each piece is well coated. Cover the bowl with plastic wrap or transfer the beef and marinade to a resealable plastic bag. Marinate the beef in the refrigerator for at least 30 minutes, or up to 2 hours for best flavor.
3. Heat a tablespoon of vegetable oil in a large skillet or grill pan over medium-high heat.
4. Remove the marinated beef from the refrigerator and let it sit at room temperature for about 10 minutes.
5. Once the skillet or grill pan is hot, add the marinated beef slices in a single layer. Cook the beef in batches if necessary, to avoid overcrowding the pan.
6. Cook the beef slices for 2-3 minutes on each side, or until they are caramelized and cooked through.

7. Transfer the cooked beef bulgogi to a serving plate or bowl. Garnish with sliced green onions and toasted sesame seeds, if desired.
8. Serve the beef bulgogi hot with steamed rice and your favorite side dishes, such as kimchi and pickled vegetables.
9. Enjoy your homemade Beef Bulgogi as a flavorful and satisfying meal!

Feel free to adjust the marinade ingredients according to your taste preferences. You can also add thinly sliced vegetables such as onions, bell peppers, and mushrooms to the marinade or cook them alongside the beef for added flavor and texture.

Thai Basil Chicken

Ingredients:

- 1 lb ground chicken
- 2 tablespoons vegetable oil
- 4 cloves garlic, minced
- 2 Thai bird's eye chilies, finely chopped (adjust to taste)
- 1 bell pepper, thinly sliced
- 1 onion, thinly sliced
- 1 cup fresh Thai basil leaves
- 2 tablespoons oyster sauce
- 1 tablespoon soy sauce
- 1 tablespoon fish sauce
- 1 teaspoon sugar
- Optional: sliced red chili for garnish
- Cooked rice, for serving

Instructions:

1. Heat the vegetable oil in a large skillet or wok over medium-high heat.
2. Add the minced garlic and chopped Thai bird's eye chilies to the skillet. Stir-fry for about 30 seconds until fragrant.
3. Add the ground chicken to the skillet, breaking it up with a spatula. Cook the chicken, stirring frequently, until it is no longer pink and starts to brown, about 5-6 minutes.
4. Add the sliced bell pepper and onion to the skillet. Stir-fry for an additional 2-3 minutes until the vegetables are tender-crisp.
5. In a small bowl, mix together the oyster sauce, soy sauce, fish sauce, and sugar. Pour the sauce mixture over the chicken and vegetables in the skillet. Stir well to combine.
6. Add the fresh Thai basil leaves to the skillet and stir-fry for another minute until the basil leaves wilt and release their aroma.
7. Taste the Thai Basil Chicken and adjust the seasoning if needed, adding more soy sauce, fish sauce, or sugar to taste.
8. Remove the skillet from heat and transfer the Thai Basil Chicken to a serving dish.
9. Garnish the Thai Basil Chicken with sliced red chili, if desired.

10. Serve the Thai Basil Chicken hot with steamed rice.
11. Enjoy your homemade Thai Basil Chicken as a flavorful and satisfying meal!

Feel free to adjust the level of spiciness by adding more or less Thai bird's eye chilies according to your taste preferences. You can also substitute the ground chicken with thinly sliced chicken breast or thigh meat if you prefer.

Steamed Dumplings

Ingredients:

For the filling:

- 1/2 lb ground pork or chicken
- 1/2 cup finely chopped cabbage
- 2 green onions, finely chopped
- 2 cloves garlic, minced
- 1 tablespoon soy sauce
- 1 tablespoon oyster sauce
- 1 teaspoon sesame oil
- 1/2 teaspoon grated ginger
- Salt and pepper, to taste

For the dumpling wrappers:

- Store-bought dumpling wrappers or homemade dumpling dough

Instructions:

1. In a mixing bowl, combine the ground pork or chicken with chopped cabbage, green onions, minced garlic, soy sauce, oyster sauce, sesame oil, grated ginger, salt, and pepper. Mix until well combined.
2. To assemble the dumplings, place a small spoonful of the filling mixture in the center of each dumpling wrapper.
3. Moisten the edges of the dumpling wrapper with water using your finger.
4. Fold the dumpling wrapper in half over the filling to create a half-moon shape. Pinch the edges together to seal the dumpling, ensuring there are no air pockets.
5. To pleat the dumplings, hold the dumpling in one hand and use the other hand to make small pleats along the sealed edge, pressing them firmly to secure.
6. Repeat the process until all the filling or wrappers are used.
7. Prepare a steamer by lining it with parchment paper or lightly greasing the steaming rack to prevent the dumplings from sticking.

8. Arrange the dumplings in the steamer, making sure they are not touching each other to prevent sticking during steaming.
9. Bring water to a boil in the steamer. Once boiling, place the steamer basket with the dumplings over the boiling water.
10. Steam the dumplings for about 10-12 minutes, or until the filling is cooked through and the dumpling wrappers are translucent and tender.
11. Carefully remove the steamed dumplings from the steamer using tongs or a spatula.
12. Serve the steamed dumplings hot with your favorite dipping sauce, such as soy sauce, chili oil, or a combination of soy sauce and rice vinegar.
13. Enjoy your homemade Steamed Dumplings as a delicious appetizer or snack!

Feel free to customize the filling by adding other ingredients such as finely chopped mushrooms, water chestnuts, or shrimp. You can also make vegetarian dumplings by using tofu or textured vegetable protein as a filling.

Korean BBQ Ribs

Ingredients:

- 2 lbs beef short ribs, cut across the bone into thin slices
- 1/2 cup soy sauce
- 1/4 cup brown sugar
- 2 tablespoons rice vinegar
- 2 tablespoons sesame oil
- 4 cloves garlic, minced
- 1 tablespoon grated ginger
- 2 green onions, chopped
- 1 tablespoon sesame seeds, toasted (for garnish)
- Optional: sliced green onions and toasted sesame seeds for garnish

Instructions:

1. In a bowl, mix together the soy sauce, brown sugar, rice vinegar, sesame oil, minced garlic, grated ginger, and chopped green onions to make the marinade.
2. Place the beef short ribs in a large resealable plastic bag or a shallow dish. Pour the marinade over the ribs, making sure they are evenly coated. Seal the bag or cover the dish with plastic wrap, and marinate the ribs in the refrigerator for at least 4 hours, or preferably overnight.
3. Preheat your grill to medium-high heat.
4. Remove the marinated ribs from the refrigerator and let them sit at room temperature for about 20-30 minutes before grilling.
5. Remove the ribs from the marinade, shaking off any excess marinade.
6. Grill the ribs on the preheated grill for 3-4 minutes on each side, or until they are cooked to your desired level of doneness and have nice grill marks.
7. Transfer the grilled ribs to a serving platter and sprinkle them with toasted sesame seeds.
8. Garnish the Korean BBQ Ribs with sliced green onions and additional toasted sesame seeds, if desired.
9. Serve the Korean BBQ Ribs hot with steamed rice and your favorite side dishes, such as kimchi and pickled vegetables.
10. Enjoy your homemade Korean BBQ Ribs as a flavorful and satisfying meal!

Feel free to adjust the sweetness or saltiness of the marinade according to your taste preferences by adding more or less brown sugar or soy sauce. You can also add a splash of mirin (Japanese sweet rice wine) for extra flavor.

Vegetable Tempura

Ingredients:

For the tempura batter:

- 1 cup all-purpose flour
- 1 tablespoon cornstarch
- 1 teaspoon baking powder
- 1 cup ice-cold water
- Pinch of salt
- Ice cubes (for chilling the water)

For the vegetables (choose any combination you like):

- Broccoli florets
- Carrot slices
- Sweet potato slices
- Bell pepper strips
- Zucchini slices
- Eggplant slices
- Mushrooms (shiitake, button, or oyster)

For frying:

- Vegetable oil, for deep frying

Instructions:

1. In a large mixing bowl, combine the all-purpose flour, cornstarch, baking powder, and a pinch of salt. Whisk together until well combined.
2. Gradually pour in the ice-cold water, stirring constantly, until the batter is smooth. Be careful not to overmix; it's okay if there are a few lumps in the batter. The key to a light and crispy tempura batter is to keep the batter cold, so make sure to use ice-cold water and keep the batter chilled until ready to use.

3. Prepare the vegetables by cutting them into bite-sized pieces or strips. Make sure they are dry before dipping them in the batter.
4. Heat vegetable oil in a deep fryer or large pot to 350°F (180°C). It's important to maintain the oil temperature throughout the frying process.
5. Dip the vegetables into the tempura batter, coating them evenly. Allow any excess batter to drip off before frying.
6. Carefully place the battered vegetables into the hot oil, making sure not to overcrowd the fryer. Fry in batches if necessary.
7. Fry the vegetables for 2-3 minutes, or until they are golden brown and crispy. Use a slotted spoon or wire mesh skimmer to remove the tempura from the oil and transfer them to a plate lined with paper towels to drain excess oil.
8. Continue frying the remaining batches of vegetables until all are cooked.
9. Serve the vegetable tempura hot with a dipping sauce, such as tempura dipping sauce (tsuyu) or tentsuyu (a mixture of soy sauce, mirin, and dashi).
10. Enjoy your homemade Vegetable Tempura as a delicious appetizer or side dish!

Feel free to experiment with different vegetables and seasonings to create your own unique tempura variations. You can also serve the tempura with a side of grated daikon radish or grated ginger for extra flavor.

Tom Yum Soup

Ingredients:

- 4 cups chicken or vegetable broth
- 1 stalk lemongrass, cut into 2-inch pieces and smashed
- 4 kaffir lime leaves, torn into pieces (optional)
- 3-4 slices galangal or ginger
- 2-3 Thai bird's eye chilies, bruised (adjust to taste)
- 2 cloves garlic, minced
- 8-10 medium-sized shrimp, peeled and deveined (optional)
- 6-8 mushrooms, sliced (such as straw mushrooms or button mushrooms)
- 1 tomato, cut into wedges
- 1 small onion, sliced
- 2 tablespoons fish sauce
- 2 tablespoons lime juice
- 1 tablespoon palm sugar or brown sugar
- 2-3 tablespoons chopped cilantro leaves
- Optional: sliced green onions and Thai basil leaves for garnish

Instructions:

1. In a large pot, bring the chicken or vegetable broth to a simmer over medium heat.
2. Add the smashed lemongrass, torn kaffir lime leaves (if using), galangal or ginger slices, bruised Thai bird's eye chilies, and minced garlic to the simmering broth. Let it simmer for about 5-10 minutes to infuse the flavors.
3. If using shrimp, add them to the broth and cook until they turn pink and opaque, about 2-3 minutes.
4. Add the sliced mushrooms, tomato wedges, and sliced onion to the soup. Let them cook for another 3-4 minutes until the vegetables are tender.
5. Season the soup with fish sauce, lime juice, and palm sugar or brown sugar. Adjust the seasoning according to your taste preferences, adding more fish sauce for saltiness, lime juice for acidity, or sugar for sweetness.
6. Stir in the chopped cilantro leaves and remove the soup from heat.
7. Ladle the Tom Yum Soup into serving bowls and garnish with sliced green onions and Thai basil leaves, if desired.

8. Serve the Tom Yum Soup hot as a flavorful and aromatic appetizer or light meal.
9. Enjoy your homemade Tom Yum Soup!

Feel free to customize your Tom Yum Soup by adding other ingredients such as tofu, chicken, or seafood. You can also adjust the spiciness of the soup by adding more or fewer Thai bird's eye chilies.

Yakisoba

Ingredients:

- 8 oz yakisoba noodles (or substitute with ramen noodles or spaghetti)
- 1 tablespoon vegetable oil
- 1 boneless, skinless chicken breast, thinly sliced (or substitute with pork, beef, shrimp, or tofu)
- 1 small onion, thinly sliced
- 1 carrot, julienned
- 1 bell pepper, thinly sliced
- 1 cup cabbage, thinly sliced
- 2 green onions, chopped
- Optional: 1 cup bean sprouts
- Optional: 1 cup sliced mushrooms (such as shiitake or button mushrooms)

For the sauce:

- 3 tablespoons soy sauce
- 2 tablespoons oyster sauce
- 1 tablespoon Worcestershire sauce
- 1 tablespoon ketchup
- 1 tablespoon sugar
- 1 teaspoon sesame oil

Instructions:

1. Cook the yakisoba noodles according to the package instructions. Drain and rinse the noodles under cold water to stop the cooking process. Set aside.
2. In a small bowl, mix together the soy sauce, oyster sauce, Worcestershire sauce, ketchup, sugar, and sesame oil to make the sauce. Set aside.
3. Heat vegetable oil in a large skillet or wok over medium-high heat.
4. Add the sliced chicken breast (or other protein of your choice) to the skillet and stir-fry until cooked through. Remove the cooked chicken from the skillet and set aside.

5. In the same skillet, add a little more oil if needed, then add the sliced onion, julienned carrot, sliced bell pepper, and sliced cabbage. Stir-fry the vegetables until they are tender-crisp, about 3-4 minutes.
6. Add the cooked yakisoba noodles to the skillet, along with the cooked chicken (or other protein), chopped green onions, bean sprouts, and sliced mushrooms (if using). Stir to combine everything together.
7. Pour the prepared sauce over the noodle and vegetable mixture in the skillet. Stir-fry for another 2-3 minutes, or until everything is heated through and well coated with the sauce.
8. Taste and adjust the seasoning if needed, adding more soy sauce or sugar to taste.
9. Remove the skillet from heat and transfer the Yakisoba to serving plates or bowls.
10. Serve the Yakisoba hot as a delicious and satisfying meal or side dish.
11. Enjoy your homemade Yakisoba!

Feel free to customize your Yakisoba by adding other vegetables such as broccoli, snow peas, or baby corn. You can also adjust the spiciness of the dish by adding a drizzle of Sriracha or chili oil.

Szechuan Beef

Ingredients:

For the beef marinade:

- 1 lb flank steak or sirloin steak, thinly sliced
- 2 tablespoons soy sauce
- 1 tablespoon rice wine or dry sherry
- 1 tablespoon cornstarch
- 1 teaspoon sesame oil
- 1 teaspoon sugar
- 1/2 teaspoon black pepper

For the stir-fry:

- 2 tablespoons vegetable oil
- 4 cloves garlic, minced
- 1 tablespoon fresh ginger, minced
- 1 bell pepper, thinly sliced
- 1 onion, thinly sliced
- 1-2 carrots, thinly sliced
- 1/2 cup sliced bamboo shoots (optional)
- 1/2 cup sliced water chestnuts (optional)
- 1/4 cup sliced green onions (for garnish)
- Sesame seeds (for garnish)

For the Szechuan sauce:

- 3 tablespoons soy sauce
- 2 tablespoons hoisin sauce
- 2 tablespoons rice vinegar
- 1 tablespoon chili garlic sauce or Szechuan sauce
- 1 tablespoon brown sugar
- 1 teaspoon sesame oil
- 1 teaspoon cornstarch mixed with 2 teaspoons water (to thicken)

Instructions:

1. In a bowl, combine the thinly sliced beef with soy sauce, rice wine or dry sherry, cornstarch, sesame oil, sugar, and black pepper. Stir until the beef is well coated in the marinade. Let it marinate for at least 15-20 minutes, or up to 1 hour in the refrigerator.
2. In a separate bowl, mix together the ingredients for the Szechuan sauce: soy sauce, hoisin sauce, rice vinegar, chili garlic sauce or Szechuan sauce, brown sugar, and sesame oil. Set aside.
3. Heat 1 tablespoon of vegetable oil in a large skillet or wok over high heat. Add the marinated beef slices in a single layer and cook for 1-2 minutes on each side until browned. Remove the beef from the skillet and set aside.
4. In the same skillet, heat another tablespoon of vegetable oil. Add minced garlic and ginger, and stir-fry for about 30 seconds until fragrant.
5. Add sliced bell pepper, onion, and carrots to the skillet. Stir-fry for 2-3 minutes until the vegetables are slightly tender.
6. Add sliced bamboo shoots and water chestnuts (if using) to the skillet and stir-fry for another minute.
7. Return the cooked beef slices to the skillet and pour the prepared Szechuan sauce over the beef and vegetables. Stir well to coat everything in the sauce.
8. Cook for another 1-2 minutes until the sauce thickens and coats the beef and vegetables evenly.
9. Garnish the Szechuan Beef with sliced green onions and sesame seeds.
10. Serve the Szechuan Beef hot with steamed rice or noodles.
11. Enjoy your homemade Szechuan Beef with its spicy and savory flavors!

Feel free to adjust the spiciness of the dish by adding more or less chili garlic sauce or Szechuan sauce according to your taste preferences. You can also add other vegetables such as broccoli, snow peas, or mushrooms to the stir-fry.

Peking Duck

Ingredients:

- 1 whole duck (about 5-6 pounds)
- 2 tablespoons honey
- 2 tablespoons soy sauce
- 1 tablespoon hoisin sauce
- 1 tablespoon Chinese five-spice powder
- 1 teaspoon salt
- 1 teaspoon pepper
- 1 teaspoon Shaoxing wine (optional)
- Thin pancakes or steamed buns
- Hoisin sauce
- Sliced cucumbers
- Sliced scallions

Instructions:

1. Clean the duck thoroughly, removing any excess fat and giblets from the cavity. Pat the duck dry with paper towels.
2. In a small bowl, mix together the honey, soy sauce, hoisin sauce, Chinese five-spice powder, salt, pepper, and Shaoxing wine (if using) to create a marinade.
3. Brush the marinade all over the duck, making sure to coat it evenly. You can also rub some of the marinade inside the cavity of the duck for extra flavor.
4. Place the duck on a rack set over a baking sheet or roasting pan, breast side up. Let the duck marinate in the refrigerator for at least 4 hours or overnight, uncovered, to allow the skin to dry out.
5. Preheat your oven to 350°F (175°C). Roast the duck for about 2-2.5 hours, or until the skin is golden brown and crispy, and the internal temperature reaches 165°F (75°C).
6. Once the duck is cooked, remove it from the oven and let it rest for 10-15 minutes before carving.
7. To serve, slice the duck thinly, including both the skin and meat. Arrange the sliced duck on a platter alongside the thin pancakes or steamed buns, hoisin sauce, sliced cucumbers, and scallions.

8. To eat, spread some hoisin sauce on a pancake or bun, add a few slices of duck, some cucumber, and scallions, then roll it up and enjoy!

Feel free to adjust the seasonings and ingredients according to your taste preferences.

Enjoy your homemade Peking duck!

Gyoza

Ingredients:

For the filling:

- 1/2 pound ground pork (you can also use chicken, turkey, or a mixture of pork and shrimp)
- 2 cups finely chopped cabbage
- 2 green onions, finely chopped
- 2 cloves garlic, minced
- 1 teaspoon fresh ginger, minced
- 2 tablespoons soy sauce
- 1 tablespoon sesame oil
- 1 teaspoon sugar
- 1/2 teaspoon salt
- 1/4 teaspoon black pepper

For assembling:

- Gyoza wrappers (you can find these in the refrigerated section of most Asian grocery stores)
- Water (for sealing)

For cooking:

- Vegetable oil
- Water

For dipping sauce:

- 2 tablespoons soy sauce
- 1 tablespoon rice vinegar
- 1 teaspoon sesame oil

- Chili oil or Sriracha (optional, for heat)

Instructions:

1. In a large mixing bowl, combine all the filling ingredients (ground pork, chopped cabbage, green onions, garlic, ginger, soy sauce, sesame oil, sugar, salt, and black pepper). Mix well until everything is evenly incorporated.
2. To assemble the gyoza, place a small spoonful of filling in the center of a gyoza wrapper. Dip your finger in water and moisten the edge of the wrapper. Fold the wrapper in half over the filling, then crimp and pleat the edges to seal the gyoza. Repeat with the remaining wrappers and filling.
3. Heat a non-stick skillet or frying pan over medium-high heat and add a tablespoon of vegetable oil.
4. Once the oil is hot, arrange the gyoza in the pan in a single layer, flat side down. Cook for 2-3 minutes, or until the bottoms are golden brown.
5. Carefully pour about 1/4 cup of water into the pan (enough to cover the bottom) and immediately cover with a lid. Steam the gyoza for 5-7 minutes, or until the wrappers are translucent and the filling is cooked through.
6. Remove the lid and continue cooking until all the water has evaporated and the bottoms of the gyoza are crispy again.
7. While the gyoza are cooking, mix together the ingredients for the dipping sauce in a small bowl.
8. Serve the gyoza hot with the dipping sauce on the side. Enjoy!

Gyoza make for a fantastic appetizer or a main course when paired with rice and a side of vegetables. Feel free to experiment with the filling ingredients to suit your taste preferences!

Thai Red Curry

Ingredients:

- 1 tablespoon vegetable oil
- 2 tablespoons Thai red curry paste (adjust to taste)
- 1 can (13.5 oz) coconut milk
- 1 cup chicken broth or vegetable broth
- 1 pound chicken breast, thinly sliced (or substitute with tofu, shrimp, or your choice of protein)
- 2 cups mixed vegetables (such as bell peppers, carrots, broccoli, snow peas, and bamboo shoots), sliced or chopped
- 2 tablespoons fish sauce (or soy sauce for a vegetarian/vegan option)
- 1 tablespoon brown sugar (optional, adjust to taste)
- Fresh basil leaves or cilantro, for garnish (optional)
- Cooked jasmine rice, for serving

Instructions:

1. Heat the vegetable oil in a large skillet or wok over medium heat. Add the Thai red curry paste and stir-fry for 1-2 minutes, until fragrant.
2. Pour in about half of the coconut milk (the thick cream part) and stir well to combine with the curry paste. Cook for another 2-3 minutes, stirring occasionally.
3. Add the sliced chicken (or your choice of protein) to the skillet and cook until it's no longer pink on the outside.
4. Pour in the remaining coconut milk and chicken broth. Bring the mixture to a simmer.
5. Add the mixed vegetables to the skillet and simmer for 5-7 minutes, or until the vegetables are tender and the chicken (if using) is cooked through.
6. Stir in the fish sauce (or soy sauce) and brown sugar, if using. Taste and adjust the seasoning as needed.
7. Remove the skillet from heat. If desired, garnish with fresh basil leaves or cilantro.
8. Serve the Thai red curry hot with cooked jasmine rice on the side.

Enjoy your homemade Thai red curry! You can customize the spice level and ingredients to suit your taste preferences. It's a versatile dish that's perfect for a cozy meal at home.

Japanese Fried Chicken (Karaage)

Ingredients:

- 1 pound boneless, skinless chicken thighs or breasts, cut into bite-sized pieces
- 3 tablespoons soy sauce
- 2 tablespoons sake (Japanese rice wine) or dry sherry
- 2 cloves garlic, minced
- 1 teaspoon grated ginger
- 1 tablespoon sesame oil
- 1 tablespoon sugar
- 1/2 cup all-purpose flour or potato starch
- Vegetable oil, for frying
- Lemon wedges, for serving (optional)
- Japanese mayonnaise or soy sauce, for dipping (optional)

Instructions:

1. In a bowl, combine the soy sauce, sake, minced garlic, grated ginger, sesame oil, and sugar to make the marinade.
2. Add the chicken pieces to the marinade and toss until well coated. Cover the bowl with plastic wrap and let the chicken marinate in the refrigerator for at least 30 minutes, or up to 4 hours for maximum flavor.
3. Heat vegetable oil in a deep fryer or large pot to 350°F (175°C).
4. Place the flour or potato starch in a shallow dish. Remove the marinated chicken from the bowl, allowing any excess marinade to drip off.
5. Dredge each piece of chicken in the flour or potato starch, shaking off any excess.
6. Carefully lower the coated chicken pieces into the hot oil, a few at a time, making sure not to overcrowd the fryer or pot. Fry the chicken in batches for about 5-7 minutes, or until golden brown and cooked through.
7. Use a slotted spoon or tongs to transfer the fried chicken to a paper towel-lined plate to drain excess oil.
8. Repeat the frying process with the remaining chicken pieces.
9. Serve the Karaage hot, with lemon wedges on the side for squeezing over the chicken, and optionally with Japanese mayonnaise or soy sauce for dipping.

Enjoy your crispy and flavorful Japanese fried chicken (Karaage)! It's perfect as a snack, appetizer, or main course served with rice and salad.

Pad See Ew

Ingredients:

- 8 ounces wide rice noodles (fresh or dried)
- 2 tablespoons vegetable oil
- 2 cloves garlic, minced
- 8 ounces sliced chicken breast, beef, shrimp, or tofu
- 2 eggs, lightly beaten
- 2 cups Chinese broccoli (gai lan) or broccoli florets
- 1/4 cup soy sauce
- 2 tablespoons oyster sauce
- 1 tablespoon fish sauce
- 1 tablespoon brown sugar
- 1/4 teaspoon ground white pepper
- Red chili flakes (optional, for spice)
- Lime wedges, for serving
- Fresh cilantro, for garnish (optional)

Instructions:

1. If using dried rice noodles, soak them in warm water for about 30 minutes until they are softened. If using fresh noodles, you can skip this step.
2. In a small bowl, mix together the soy sauce, oyster sauce, fish sauce, brown sugar, and ground white pepper to make the sauce. Set aside.
3. Heat 1 tablespoon of vegetable oil in a large wok or skillet over medium-high heat. Add the minced garlic and stir-fry for about 30 seconds until fragrant.
4. Add the sliced chicken, beef, shrimp, or tofu to the wok and stir-fry until cooked through. If using tofu, fry until golden brown on both sides. Remove the cooked protein from the wok and set aside.
5. In the same wok, heat the remaining tablespoon of vegetable oil. Add the beaten eggs and scramble until just set.
6. Add the Chinese broccoli (or broccoli florets) to the wok and stir-fry for 2-3 minutes, or until they are tender-crisp.
7. Push the vegetables to one side of the wok and add the soaked rice noodles to the other side. Pour the sauce over the noodles and toss everything together until the noodles are evenly coated with the sauce.

8. Return the cooked protein to the wok and stir-fry everything together for another 2-3 minutes, or until heated through.
9. Taste and adjust the seasoning, adding more soy sauce or fish sauce if needed. If you like your Pad See Ew spicy, you can add red chili flakes at this point.
10. Serve the Pad See Ew hot, garnished with fresh cilantro and lime wedges on the side for squeezing over the noodles.

Enjoy your homemade Pad See Ew! It's a comforting and satisfying dish that's perfect for lunch or dinner.

Okonomiyaki

Ingredients:

For the batter:

- 1 cup all-purpose flour
- 1 cup dashi stock (or substitute with water or chicken/vegetable broth)
- 2 eggs
- 2 cups shredded cabbage
- 2 green onions, thinly sliced
- 1/4 cup tenkasu (tempura scraps, optional)
- 1/4 cup pickled red ginger (beni shoga, optional)
- Salt and pepper, to taste

For the toppings (optional):

- Thinly sliced pork belly, shrimp, squid, or other protein of your choice
- Okonomiyaki sauce (or substitute with Worcestershire sauce mixed with ketchup)
- Japanese mayonnaise
- Aonori (dried green seaweed flakes)
- Katsuobushi (bonito flakes)
- Pickled ginger (gari)
- Toasted sesame seeds

Instructions:

1. In a large mixing bowl, whisk together the flour, dashi stock, and eggs until smooth.
2. Add the shredded cabbage, green onions, tenkasu (if using), pickled red ginger (if using), and season with salt and pepper. Mix until everything is well combined and coated in the batter.
3. Heat a non-stick skillet or griddle over medium heat. If using thinly sliced pork belly or other protein, place it on the skillet and cook until browned and partially cooked.

4. Pour a ladleful of the okonomiyaki batter onto the skillet, spreading it out into a round pancake shape, about 1/2 to 3/4 inch thick.
5. Cook the okonomiyaki for 4-5 minutes on one side, or until the bottom is golden brown and crispy.
6. Carefully flip the okonomiyaki using a spatula, and continue cooking for another 4-5 minutes on the other side, or until golden brown and cooked through.
7. Once cooked, transfer the okonomiyaki to a serving plate.
8. Drizzle okonomiyaki sauce and Japanese mayonnaise over the top of the okonomiyaki in a crisscross pattern.
9. Sprinkle with aonori (dried seaweed flakes), katsuobushi (bonito flakes), and toasted sesame seeds.
10. Serve the okonomiyaki hot, cut into wedges, with pickled ginger on the side.

Enjoy your homemade okonomiyaki! It's a delightful and customizable dish that's perfect for sharing with friends and family.

Sweet and Sour Chicken

Ingredients:

For the chicken:

- 1 pound boneless, skinless chicken breasts or thighs, cut into bite-sized pieces
- 1/2 cup cornstarch
- 2 eggs, beaten
- Salt and pepper, to taste
- Vegetable oil, for frying

For the sauce:

- 1/2 cup ketchup
- 1/4 cup rice vinegar
- 1/4 cup brown sugar
- 2 tablespoons soy sauce
- 1 tablespoon cornstarch
- 1/4 cup water

For stir-frying:

- 1 tablespoon vegetable oil
- 1 bell pepper, cut into chunks
- 1 onion, cut into chunks
- 1 cup pineapple chunks (fresh or canned)
- Optional garnish: sliced green onions, sesame seeds

Instructions:

1. Start by preparing the chicken. Season the chicken pieces with salt and pepper. Dip each piece into the beaten eggs, then dredge in cornstarch, ensuring they are evenly coated.

2. Heat vegetable oil in a large skillet or wok over medium-high heat for frying. Once the oil is hot, carefully add the coated chicken pieces in batches, frying until golden brown and cooked through. Remove the cooked chicken pieces from the oil and place them on a paper towel-lined plate to drain excess oil. Set aside.
3. In a small bowl, whisk together the ketchup, rice vinegar, brown sugar, soy sauce, cornstarch, and water to make the sauce. Set aside.
4. In the same skillet or wok used to fry the chicken, heat 1 tablespoon of vegetable oil over medium-high heat. Add the bell pepper and onion chunks, and stir-fry for 2-3 minutes, or until they start to soften.
5. Add the pineapple chunks to the skillet and continue to stir-fry for another 1-2 minutes.
6. Pour the prepared sweet and sour sauce into the skillet with the vegetables. Stir well and bring the sauce to a simmer.
7. Add the fried chicken pieces to the skillet, tossing them in the sauce until they are evenly coated.
8. Continue to cook for another 2-3 minutes, or until the sauce has thickened and the chicken is heated through.
9. Remove the skillet from heat. Garnish with sliced green onions and sesame seeds, if desired.
10. Serve the sweet and sour chicken hot with steamed rice or noodles.

Enjoy your homemade sweet and sour chicken! It's a delicious and satisfying dish that's sure to please everyone at the dinner table.

Vietnamese Spring Rolls

Ingredients:

For the spring rolls:

- Rice paper wrappers (banh trang)
- 8-10 large shrimp, cooked, peeled, and halved lengthwise
- 8-10 rice paper wrappers
- 2 cups cooked rice vermicelli noodles, cooled
- 1 cup thinly sliced lettuce or mixed salad greens
- 1 cup thinly sliced cucumber
- 1 cup matchstick-cut carrots
- 1 cup fresh herbs (such as cilantro, Thai basil, mint, or a combination)
- Optional: cooked chicken breast strips, tofu strips, or shredded cooked pork

For the dipping sauce:

- 1/4 cup hoisin sauce
- 2 tablespoons peanut butter
- 1-2 tablespoons water, as needed
- 1 tablespoon soy sauce
- 1 tablespoon lime juice
- 1 teaspoon sriracha sauce (optional, for heat)
- Crushed peanuts, for garnish (optional)

Instructions:

1. Prepare all the filling ingredients and have them ready for assembling the spring rolls.
2. Fill a large shallow dish or pie plate with warm water. Dip one rice paper wrapper into the water and rotate it gently for about 10-15 seconds, or until it softens and becomes pliable. Be careful not to over-soak the rice paper, as it will become too soft and difficult to handle.
3. Lay the softened rice paper wrapper flat on a clean work surface, such as a cutting board or plate.

4. Arrange a small handful of cooked rice vermicelli noodles in the center of the rice paper wrapper, leaving some space on the sides.
5. Layer the lettuce, cucumber, carrots, fresh herbs, and protein (if using) on top of the rice noodles.
6. Fold the bottom edge of the rice paper wrapper over the filling, then fold in the sides, and roll tightly to enclose the filling. Repeat with the remaining ingredients.
7. Place the finished spring rolls on a serving platter, seam side down, and cover them with a damp kitchen towel to keep them from drying out while you assemble the rest.
8. To make the dipping sauce, whisk together the hoisin sauce, peanut butter, water (as needed to thin the sauce to your desired consistency), soy sauce, lime juice, and sriracha sauce (if using) until smooth. Adjust the seasoning to taste.
9. Serve the Vietnamese spring rolls with the dipping sauce on the side. Garnish with crushed peanuts, if desired.

Enjoy your homemade Vietnamese spring rolls! They make a refreshing appetizer, light lunch, or healthy snack. Feel free to customize the filling ingredients according to your taste preferences.

Bibim Guksu

Ingredients:

For the noodles and vegetables:

- 8 ounces somyeon (thin wheat noodles)
- 1 cup julienned cucumber
- 1 cup julienned carrot
- 1 cup julienned red bell pepper
- 1 cup julienned Korean pear or apple (optional)
- 1 cup shredded lettuce or mixed salad greens
- 2 green onions, thinly sliced
- 1/4 cup chopped fresh cilantro or parsley (optional)
- Toasted sesame seeds, for garnish

For the sauce:

- 3 tablespoons gochujang (Korean red chili paste)
- 2 tablespoons rice vinegar
- 2 tablespoons soy sauce
- 1 tablespoon sesame oil
- 1 tablespoon honey or sugar
- 2 cloves garlic, minced
- 1 teaspoon grated ginger
- 1 teaspoon toasted sesame seeds
- 1 tablespoon water, as needed

Instructions:

1. Cook the somyeon noodles according to the package instructions until they are al dente. Drain and rinse the noodles under cold running water to stop the cooking process and cool them down. Set aside.
2. Prepare the vegetables by julienning the cucumber, carrot, red bell pepper, and Korean pear or apple (if using). You can also shred the lettuce or mixed salad greens. Arrange the vegetables on a serving platter.

3. In a small bowl, whisk together the ingredients for the sauce: gochujang, rice vinegar, soy sauce, sesame oil, honey or sugar, minced garlic, grated ginger, toasted sesame seeds, and water (as needed to adjust the consistency). Taste the sauce and adjust the seasoning if needed.
4. To assemble the Bibim Guksu, place a portion of the cooked and cooled noodles in a serving bowl. Top with a generous amount of the julienned vegetables, green onions, and chopped cilantro or parsley (if using).
5. Drizzle the spicy sauce over the noodles and vegetables, using as much or as little as you prefer. Toss everything together until well combined and evenly coated with the sauce.
6. Sprinkle toasted sesame seeds over the top for garnish.
7. Serve the Bibim Guksu immediately, or refrigerate for a while to allow the flavors to meld before serving.

Enjoy your homemade Bibim Guksu! It's a refreshing and satisfying dish that's perfect for lunch or dinner. Feel free to adjust the spiciness level and add any other vegetables or toppings you like.

Chicken Satay

Ingredients:

For the chicken:

- 1 pound boneless, skinless chicken breasts or thighs, cut into thin strips
- 1/4 cup coconut milk
- 2 tablespoons soy sauce
- 2 tablespoons fish sauce
- 1 tablespoon brown sugar
- 1 tablespoon curry powder
- 2 cloves garlic, minced
- 1 tablespoon grated ginger
- Wooden skewers, soaked in water for at least 30 minutes

For the peanut sauce:

- 1/2 cup creamy peanut butter
- 1/4 cup coconut milk
- 2 tablespoons soy sauce
- 1 tablespoon brown sugar
- 1 tablespoon lime juice
- 1 teaspoon grated ginger
- 1 clove garlic, minced
- 1/4 teaspoon red pepper flakes (optional, for heat)
- Water, as needed to adjust consistency

Instructions:

1. In a bowl, whisk together the coconut milk, soy sauce, fish sauce, brown sugar, curry powder, minced garlic, and grated ginger to make the marinade for the chicken.
2. Add the chicken strips to the marinade and toss until well coated. Cover the bowl and refrigerate for at least 1 hour, or up to overnight, to allow the flavors to meld.

3. While the chicken is marinating, prepare the peanut sauce. In a small saucepan, combine the peanut butter, coconut milk, soy sauce, brown sugar, lime juice, grated ginger, minced garlic, and red pepper flakes (if using). Heat over low heat, stirring constantly, until the sauce is smooth and creamy. If the sauce is too thick, you can thin it out with a little water. Remove from heat and set aside.
4. Preheat a grill or grill pan over medium-high heat. Thread the marinated chicken strips onto the soaked wooden skewers.
5. Grill the chicken skewers for 3-4 minutes on each side, or until cooked through and slightly charred. Be careful not to overcook the chicken to keep it moist and tender.
6. Once the chicken is cooked, transfer the skewers to a serving platter.
7. Serve the chicken satay hot with the peanut sauce on the side for dipping.
8. Optionally, garnish with chopped peanuts and chopped cilantro for extra flavor and presentation.

Enjoy your homemade chicken satay with peanut sauce! It's a crowd-pleasing appetizer or main course that's perfect for parties or family dinners.

Tom Kha Gai

Ingredients:

- 1 pound boneless, skinless chicken breasts or thighs, thinly sliced
- 4 cups chicken broth
- 1 can (14 oz) coconut milk
- 8-10 kaffir lime leaves, torn into pieces
- 2 stalks lemongrass, bruised and chopped into 2-inch pieces
- 3-4 slices galangal (or substitute with ginger)
- 8 ounces mushrooms (such as straw mushrooms or button mushrooms), sliced
- 2 tablespoons fish sauce
- 2 tablespoons lime juice
- 1-2 Thai bird's eye chilies, thinly sliced (adjust to taste)
- 2 tablespoons chopped cilantro leaves, for garnish
- Thinly sliced green onions, for garnish

Instructions:

1. In a large pot, bring the chicken broth to a boil over medium-high heat.
2. Add the torn kaffir lime leaves, chopped lemongrass, and galangal slices to the pot. Reduce the heat to medium-low and simmer for about 5 minutes to infuse the broth with the aromatic flavors.
3. Add the sliced chicken to the pot and simmer for another 5-7 minutes, or until the chicken is cooked through.
4. Stir in the coconut milk and sliced mushrooms. Simmer for an additional 3-4 minutes, or until the mushrooms are tender.
5. Season the soup with fish sauce and lime juice, adjusting the seasoning to taste. If you prefer a spicier soup, add thinly sliced Thai bird's eye chilies.
6. Once the soup is seasoned to your liking, remove the pot from heat.
7. Ladle the Tom Kha Gai into serving bowls. Garnish with chopped cilantro leaves and thinly sliced green onions.
8. Serve the soup hot as an appetizer or as a main course with steamed rice.

Enjoy your homemade Tom Kha Gai! It's a comforting and flavorful Thai soup that's perfect for warming up on chilly days or for enjoying any time of the year.

Teriyaki Tofu

Ingredients:

For the tofu:

- 1 block (14-16 ounces) extra-firm tofu
- 2 tablespoons soy sauce
- 2 tablespoons mirin (Japanese sweet rice wine)
- 1 tablespoon rice vinegar
- 1 tablespoon honey or maple syrup
- 1 teaspoon grated ginger
- 1 clove garlic, minced
- 1 tablespoon vegetable oil, for cooking

For the teriyaki sauce:

- 1/4 cup soy sauce
- 2 tablespoons mirin
- 2 tablespoons honey or maple syrup
- 1 teaspoon rice vinegar
- 1 teaspoon grated ginger
- 1 clove garlic, minced
- 1 teaspoon cornstarch (optional, to thicken the sauce)
- 1 tablespoon water (if using cornstarch)

Instructions:

1. Press the tofu: Drain the tofu and wrap it in paper towels or a clean kitchen towel. Place a heavy object, such as a cast-iron skillet or a couple of canned goods, on top of the tofu and let it press for about 30 minutes to remove excess water.
2. While the tofu is pressing, prepare the marinade. In a shallow dish, whisk together the soy sauce, mirin, rice vinegar, honey or maple syrup, grated ginger, and minced garlic.
3. Once the tofu has been pressed, cut it into cubes or slices of your desired size.

4. Place the tofu pieces in the marinade and let them marinate for at least 15-30 minutes, flipping them halfway through to ensure even coating.
5. While the tofu is marinating, prepare the teriyaki sauce. In a small saucepan, combine the soy sauce, mirin, honey or maple syrup, rice vinegar, grated ginger, and minced garlic. If you prefer a thicker sauce, mix the cornstarch with water in a separate small bowl until smooth, then add it to the saucepan.
6. Bring the sauce to a simmer over medium heat, stirring frequently. Cook for 2-3 minutes, or until the sauce has thickened slightly. Remove from heat and set aside.
7. Heat the vegetable oil in a large skillet or non-stick pan over medium-high heat. Once the oil is hot, add the marinated tofu pieces in a single layer, reserving any leftover marinade.
8. Cook the tofu for 3-4 minutes on each side, or until golden brown and crispy. Use a spatula to gently flip the tofu pieces halfway through cooking.
9. Once the tofu is cooked, pour the reserved marinade into the skillet with the tofu. Cook for another minute, allowing the marinade to thicken and coat the tofu.
10. Remove the skillet from heat and drizzle the teriyaki sauce over the tofu. Toss gently to coat the tofu evenly with the sauce.
11. Serve the teriyaki tofu hot with steamed rice and your favorite vegetables. Garnish with sesame seeds and sliced green onions, if desired.

Enjoy your homemade teriyaki tofu! It's a delicious and satisfying vegetarian dish packed with flavor.

Chicken Yakitori

Ingredients:

For the chicken:

- 1 pound boneless, skinless chicken thighs or breasts, cut into bite-sized pieces
- Bamboo skewers, soaked in water for at least 30 minutes

For the yakitori sauce:

- 1/4 cup soy sauce
- 1/4 cup mirin (Japanese sweet rice wine)
- 2 tablespoons sake (Japanese rice wine) or dry sherry
- 2 tablespoons brown sugar
- 2 cloves garlic, minced
- 1 teaspoon grated ginger
- 1 tablespoon honey or maple syrup (optional, for extra sweetness)
- Toasted sesame seeds, for garnish
- Thinly sliced green onions, for garnish

Instructions:

1. In a small saucepan, combine the soy sauce, mirin, sake, brown sugar, minced garlic, and grated ginger to make the yakitori sauce. If you prefer a sweeter sauce, you can add honey or maple syrup to taste. Bring the sauce to a simmer over medium heat, stirring occasionally, until the sugar is dissolved and the sauce has slightly thickened. Remove from heat and set aside to cool.
2. While the sauce is cooling, prepare the chicken skewers. Thread the chicken pieces onto the soaked bamboo skewers, leaving a little space between each piece.
3. Preheat a grill or grill pan over medium-high heat. Lightly oil the grill grates to prevent sticking.
4. Once the grill is hot, place the chicken skewers on the grill and cook for 3-4 minutes on each side, or until the chicken is cooked through and nicely charred

on the outside. Brush the chicken skewers with the yakitori sauce during the last few minutes of cooking, turning occasionally to coat evenly.
5. Once the chicken is cooked, remove the skewers from the grill and transfer them to a serving platter.
6. Brush the cooked chicken skewers with any remaining yakitori sauce and sprinkle with toasted sesame seeds and thinly sliced green onions for garnish.
7. Serve the chicken yakitori hot as an appetizer or main course, along with steamed rice and your favorite vegetables.

Enjoy your homemade chicken yakitori! It's a delicious and flavorful dish that's perfect for grilling season or any time you're craving Japanese-inspired flavors.

Thai Peanut Noodles

Ingredients:

For the noodles:

- 8 ounces spaghetti or linguine noodles
- 1 tablespoon sesame oil (or vegetable oil)

For the peanut sauce:

- 1/3 cup creamy peanut butter
- 3 tablespoons soy sauce
- 2 tablespoons rice vinegar
- 2 tablespoons honey or maple syrup
- 1 tablespoon sesame oil
- 1 tablespoon lime juice
- 1 clove garlic, minced
- 1 teaspoon grated ginger
- 1/4 teaspoon red pepper flakes (adjust to taste)
- 1/4 cup warm water, or more as needed to thin the sauce

For serving (optional):

- Thinly sliced green onions
- Chopped cilantro
- Crushed peanuts
- Lime wedges

Instructions:

1. Cook the noodles according to the package instructions until al dente. Drain the noodles and rinse them under cold water to stop the cooking process. Toss the noodles with 1 tablespoon of sesame oil to prevent sticking and set aside.

2. In a medium bowl, whisk together the peanut butter, soy sauce, rice vinegar, honey or maple syrup, sesame oil, lime juice, minced garlic, grated ginger, and red pepper flakes until smooth. If the sauce is too thick, gradually add warm water, a tablespoon at a time, until you reach your desired consistency. The sauce should be creamy and pourable.
3. Pour the peanut sauce over the cooked noodles and toss until the noodles are evenly coated with the sauce.
4. Taste and adjust the seasoning, adding more soy sauce for saltiness, lime juice for acidity, or honey/maple syrup for sweetness, according to your preference.
5. Transfer the Thai peanut noodles to serving plates or a serving bowl.
6. Garnish the noodles with thinly sliced green onions, chopped cilantro, crushed peanuts, and lime wedges, if desired.
7. Serve the Thai peanut noodles immediately at room temperature or chilled, as they can be enjoyed both ways.

Enjoy your homemade Thai peanut noodles! They're perfect as a standalone meal or as a side dish, and they can be customized with your favorite vegetables or proteins, such as tofu, chicken, shrimp, or edamame.

Korean Japchae

Ingredients:

- 6 ounces Korean glass noodles (dangmyeon)
- 2 tablespoons vegetable oil
- 2 cloves garlic, minced
- 1 small onion, thinly sliced
- 1 carrot, julienned
- 1 red bell pepper, julienned
- 4 ounces spinach, washed and trimmed
- 4 ounces mushrooms (shiitake, oyster, or button), sliced
- 2 green onions, thinly sliced
- 2 tablespoons soy sauce
- 1 tablespoon sesame oil
- 1 tablespoon sugar
- Toasted sesame seeds, for garnish
- Optional: cooked beef, pork, chicken, or tofu, sliced into thin strips

Instructions:

1. Cook the glass noodles according to the package instructions until they are soft and translucent. Drain the noodles and rinse them under cold water to stop the cooking process. Set aside.
2. Heat 1 tablespoon of vegetable oil in a large skillet or wok over medium heat. Add the minced garlic and sliced onion, and sauté until the onion is translucent.
3. Add the julienned carrot and red bell pepper to the skillet, and continue to stir-fry for 2-3 minutes, or until the vegetables are tender-crisp.
4. Push the cooked vegetables to one side of the skillet, and add the remaining tablespoon of vegetable oil to the empty space. Add the sliced mushrooms to the skillet and stir-fry until they are softened and browned.
5. Add the spinach to the skillet and stir-fry until wilted. If using cooked meat or tofu, add it to the skillet at this point and toss with the vegetables.
6. In a small bowl, mix together the soy sauce, sesame oil, and sugar to make the seasoning sauce.
7. Add the cooked glass noodles to the skillet, along with the sliced green onions. Pour the seasoning sauce over the noodles and vegetables.

8. Stir-fry everything together until the noodles are evenly coated with the sauce and heated through.
9. Remove the skillet from heat and transfer the Japchae to a serving platter.
10. Garnish the Japchae with toasted sesame seeds.
11. Serve the Japchae hot or at room temperature as a side dish or main course.

Enjoy your homemade Korean Japchae! It's a delightful dish that's perfect for any occasion, whether it's a family dinner or a gathering with friends.

Ramen Burger

Ingredients:

For the ramen buns:

- 2 packs of instant ramen noodles (discard the seasoning packets)
- 2 large eggs, beaten
- 2 tablespoons vegetable oil, for frying

For the burger patties:

- 1 pound ground beef (or substitute with ground chicken, turkey, pork, or a vegetarian option)
- Salt and pepper, to taste
- 2 tablespoons soy sauce
- 1 tablespoon sesame oil
- 1 teaspoon grated ginger
- 1 clove garlic, minced

For assembling the burgers:

- Sliced cheese (cheddar, American, Swiss, or your favorite variety)
- Burger toppings of your choice (lettuce, tomato, onion, pickles, etc.)
- Condiments (mayonnaise, ketchup, mustard, etc.)

Instructions:

1. Cook the instant ramen noodles according to the package instructions, but slightly undercook them to ensure they hold together better when forming the buns. Drain the cooked noodles and rinse them under cold water to stop the cooking process. Let the noodles cool slightly.
2. In a large mixing bowl, combine the cooked ramen noodles with the beaten eggs. Mix until the noodles are evenly coated with the eggs.

3. Divide the noodle mixture into four equal portions. Using a round mold or your hands, shape each portion into a round patty, about the same size as a burger bun. Make sure the patties are firmly packed together.
4. Heat vegetable oil in a large skillet or griddle over medium heat. Once the oil is hot, carefully place the ramen noodle patties in the skillet. Cook for 3-4 minutes on each side, or until golden brown and crispy. Remove the cooked ramen buns from the skillet and set aside.
5. In a separate mixing bowl, combine the ground beef with soy sauce, sesame oil, grated ginger, minced garlic, salt, and pepper. Mix until the seasonings are evenly incorporated into the meat. Divide the seasoned meat into four equal portions and shape them into burger patties.
6. Heat a grill or grill pan over medium-high heat. Grill the burger patties for 3-4 minutes on each side, or until they reach your desired level of doneness. During the last minute of cooking, place a slice of cheese on each burger patty to melt.
7. To assemble the Ramen Burgers, place a cooked ramen noodle patty on a plate. Top with a grilled burger patty with melted cheese, followed by your desired burger toppings and condiments. Finally, place another ramen noodle patty on top to complete the burger.
8. Serve the Ramen Burgers immediately, and enjoy the unique combination of flavors and textures!

Feel free to customize your Ramen Burger with your favorite burger toppings and condiments to suit your taste preferences. It's a fun and creative twist on the classic burger that's sure to impress your friends and family!

Stir-Fried Noodles

Ingredients:

8 ounces of your favorite noodles (such as spaghetti, linguine, rice noodles, or egg noodles)

2 tablespoons vegetable oil

2 cloves garlic, minced

1 small onion, thinly sliced

1 bell pepper, thinly sliced

1 carrot, julienned

2 cups mixed vegetables (such as broccoli florets, snap peas, sliced mushrooms, or baby corn)

2 cups protein of your choice (sliced chicken, beef, shrimp, tofu, or a combination)

Salt and pepper, to taste

Stir-fry sauce (see recipe below)

Optional garnishes: chopped green onions, sesame seeds, chopped cilantro, sliced chili peppers

For the stir-fry sauce:

1/4 cup soy sauce

2 tablespoons oyster sauce

1 tablespoon hoisin sauce

1 tablespoon rice vinegar

1 tablespoon brown sugar

1 teaspoon sesame oil

1 teaspoon grated ginger

1 teaspoon cornstarch (optional, to thicken the sauce)

2 tablespoons water (if using cornstarch)

Instructions:

Cook the noodles according to the package instructions until they are al dente. Drain the noodles and rinse them under cold water to stop the cooking process. Set aside.

In a small bowl, whisk together all the ingredients for the stir-fry sauce until well combined. Set aside.

Heat vegetable oil in a large skillet or wok over medium-high heat. Add minced garlic and thinly sliced onions to the skillet and stir-fry for 1-2 minutes until fragrant.

Add the sliced bell pepper, julienned carrot, and any other hard vegetables (such as broccoli or baby corn) to the skillet. Stir-fry for another 3-4 minutes until the vegetables are slightly softened.

Push the vegetables to one side of the skillet and add the protein of your choice to the empty space. Stir-fry until the protein is cooked through.

Add the cooked noodles to the skillet, along with the mixed vegetables and stir-fry sauce. Toss everything together until the noodles and vegetables are evenly coated with the sauce.

Continue to stir-fry for another 2-3 minutes, or until the noodles are heated through and the sauce has thickened slightly. Season with salt and pepper to taste.

Remove the skillet from heat and transfer the stir-fried noodles to serving plates.

Garnish with chopped green onions, sesame seeds, chopped cilantro, and sliced chili peppers, if desired.

Serve the stir-fried noodles hot, and enjoy!

Feel free to customize your stir-fried noodles with your favorite ingredients and adjust the seasoning to suit your taste preferences. It's a quick and easy dish that's perfect for a weeknight dinner or a casual gathering with friends and family!

Malaysian Laksa

Ingredients:

For the Laksa Paste:

- 6 dried red chilies, soaked in hot water for 15 minutes
- 4 shallots, peeled
- 3 cloves garlic, peeled
- 1-inch piece of ginger, peeled
- 1-inch piece of galangal, peeled
- 2 stalks lemongrass, tough outer layers removed and chopped
- 1 tablespoon ground coriander
- 1 tablespoon ground cumin
- 1 teaspoon ground turmeric
- 1 tablespoon shrimp paste (belacan)
- 2 tablespoons vegetable oil

For the Laksa Soup:

- 4 cups chicken or vegetable broth
- 1 can (14 oz) coconut milk
- 2 tablespoons fish sauce
- 1 tablespoon brown sugar
- Salt to taste

For the Toppings:

- 8 oz rice vermicelli noodles, cooked according to package instructions
- Cooked protein of your choice (shrimp, chicken, tofu, etc.)
- Hard-boiled eggs, halved
- Bean sprouts
- Fresh cilantro leaves
- Lime wedges
- Sambal or chili paste (optional)

Instructions:

1. Make the Laksa Paste: In a blender or food processor, combine the soaked dried chilies, shallots, garlic, ginger, galangal, lemongrass, ground coriander, ground cumin, ground turmeric, and shrimp paste. Blend until smooth.
2. Heat the vegetable oil in a large pot over medium heat. Add the Laksa paste and cook for 5-7 minutes, stirring constantly, until fragrant.
3. Pour in the chicken or vegetable broth and bring to a simmer. Let it simmer for about 10 minutes to allow the flavors to meld.
4. Stir in the coconut milk, fish sauce, and brown sugar. Season with salt to taste. Let the soup simmer for another 5 minutes.
5. Prepare the toppings: Cook the rice vermicelli noodles according to package instructions. Cook the protein of your choice (shrimp, chicken, tofu, etc.) if not already cooked. Hard-boil the eggs and halve them.
6. To serve, divide the cooked noodles among serving bowls. Ladle the hot Laksa soup over the noodles.
7. Arrange the cooked protein, halved hard-boiled eggs, bean sprouts, and fresh cilantro leaves on top of the soup.
8. Serve the Laksa Lemak hot, with lime wedges and sambal or chili paste on the side for extra flavor and heat.

Enjoy your homemade Malaysian Laksa Lemak! It's a comforting and aromatic dish that's perfect for any occasion. Feel free to adjust the toppings and spice level according to your preference.

Korean Kimchi

Ingredients:

- 1 medium-sized napa cabbage (about 2 pounds)
- 1/4 cup coarse sea salt
- 4 cups water
- 1 Korean radish (daikon), peeled and cut into matchsticks
- 4-5 green onions, chopped into 2-inch pieces
- 1/4 cup Korean chili powder (gochugaru)
- 1 tablespoon fish sauce (or soy sauce for vegetarian option)
- 1 tablespoon minced garlic
- 1 teaspoon grated ginger
- 1 teaspoon sugar
- Optional: 1 tablespoon salted shrimp or fish sauce (for extra flavor)
- Optional: 1/2 cup carrot, julienned (for added crunch and sweetness)

Instructions:

1. Prepare the cabbage: Cut the napa cabbage in half lengthwise, then cut each half into quarters. Remove the core from each quarter. Chop the cabbage into bite-sized pieces.
2. In a large bowl, dissolve the coarse sea salt in water to make a brine. Submerge the chopped cabbage in the brine and let it soak for 1-2 hours, turning occasionally to ensure even salting. Drain the cabbage and rinse it under cold water to remove excess salt. Drain well and set aside.
3. In a separate large bowl, combine the chopped radish, green onions, Korean chili powder, fish sauce (or soy sauce), minced garlic, grated ginger, and sugar. If using salted shrimp or fish sauce, add it to the mixture as well.
4. Add the drained cabbage and optional julienned carrots to the bowl with the seasoning mixture. Use your hands to mix and massage the seasoning into the vegetables, ensuring they are evenly coated.
5. Pack the seasoned cabbage mixture tightly into a clean glass jar or container, pressing down firmly to remove any air pockets. Leave some space at the top of the jar to allow for expansion during fermentation.
6. Cover the jar loosely with a lid or plastic wrap to allow gases to escape during fermentation. Place the jar in a cool, dark place, such as a pantry or cupboard, and let it ferment at room temperature for 1-5 days, depending on your

preference for fermentation level and taste. Check the kimchi daily and press down on the vegetables to submerge them in their brine.
7. Once the kimchi reaches your desired level of fermentation, transfer the jar to the refrigerator to slow down the fermentation process and chill the kimchi. It will continue to develop flavor over time in the refrigerator.
8. Serve Korean Kimchi as a side dish with rice, noodles, or as a topping for various Korean dishes. Enjoy its tangy, spicy, and complex flavor!

Note: Homemade kimchi will continue to ferment over time, developing more sour and tangy flavors. It can be stored in the refrigerator for several weeks to several months, depending on personal preference and fermentation level.

Singaporean Chili Crab

Ingredients:

For the crab:

- 2 large mud crabs (about 2-3 pounds each), cleaned and cut into pieces
- 2 tablespoons vegetable oil
- 4 cloves garlic, minced
- 1-inch piece of ginger, grated
- 2 red chilies, sliced
- 1 green chili, sliced
- 2 stalks lemongrass, bruised and chopped
- 1/2 cup chicken or seafood stock
- Salt and pepper to taste
- Chopped cilantro or green onions for garnish

For the chili crab sauce:

- 1/4 cup ketchup
- 2 tablespoons soy sauce
- 2 tablespoons chili sauce or sambal oelek
- 2 tablespoons tomato paste
- 1 tablespoon brown sugar or palm sugar
- 1 tablespoon tamarind paste (or substitute with lime juice)
- 1 tablespoon fish sauce
- 1 teaspoon sesame oil
- 1/2 cup water
- 1 tablespoon cornstarch mixed with 2 tablespoons water (optional, for thickening)

Instructions:

1. In a large wok or skillet, heat the vegetable oil over medium heat. Add the minced garlic, grated ginger, sliced red chilies, green chilies, and chopped lemongrass. Stir-fry for 1-2 minutes until fragrant.

2. Add the crab pieces to the wok and stir-fry for another 2-3 minutes, coating them with the aromatics.
3. Pour in the chicken or seafood stock and season with salt and pepper to taste. Cover the wok and let the crabs simmer for about 8-10 minutes until they are cooked through.
4. In the meantime, prepare the chili crab sauce. In a bowl, mix together the ketchup, soy sauce, chili sauce or sambal oelek, tomato paste, brown sugar, tamarind paste, fish sauce, sesame oil, and water.
5. Once the crabs are cooked, pour the chili crab sauce over them in the wok. Stir to coat the crabs evenly with the sauce. If you prefer a thicker sauce, you can add the cornstarch mixture and stir until the sauce thickens.
6. Continue to cook the crabs in the sauce for another 2-3 minutes, stirring occasionally, until the sauce is heated through and the crabs are well coated.
7. Transfer the Singaporean Chili Crab to a serving platter. Garnish with chopped cilantro or green onions.
8. Serve the chili crab hot with steamed rice or crusty bread to soak up the delicious sauce.

Enjoy your homemade Singaporean Chili Crab! It's a flavorful and satisfying dish that's perfect for seafood lovers and special occasions.

Japanese Tempura

Ingredients:

For the tempura batter:

- 1 cup all-purpose flour
- 1/2 cup cornstarch
- 1 teaspoon baking powder
- 1 cup ice-cold water
- 1 egg, beaten
- Ice cubes

For the tempura ingredients:

- Assorted seafood (shrimp, squid, fish fillets) and vegetables (zucchini, sweet potato, bell peppers, mushrooms, broccoli florets, etc.), cleaned and cut into bite-sized pieces
- Vegetable oil, for deep-frying
- Salt, for seasoning

For serving (optional):

- Tempura dipping sauce (Tentsuyu), made from equal parts soy sauce, mirin, and dashi broth, seasoned with a touch of sugar
- Grated daikon radish
- Grated ginger
- Shichimi togarashi (Japanese seven spice blend)
- Steamed rice

Instructions:

1. Prepare the tempura batter: In a large mixing bowl, combine the all-purpose flour, cornstarch, and baking powder. Whisk together to combine. In a separate bowl,

beat the egg and add the ice-cold water. Gradually pour the wet ingredients into the dry ingredients, whisking gently until just combined. Do not overmix; it's okay if there are lumps. Place a few ice cubes in the batter to keep it cold while you prepare the ingredients.
2. Prepare the tempura ingredients: Clean and cut the seafood and vegetables into bite-sized pieces. Pat them dry with paper towels to remove excess moisture, which helps the batter adhere better.
3. Heat vegetable oil in a deep fryer or large pot to 350-375°F (180-190°C).
4. Dip the seafood and vegetables into the tempura batter, coating them evenly. Allow any excess batter to drip off.
5. Carefully place the coated ingredients into the hot oil, a few pieces at a time, to avoid overcrowding the fryer. Fry until golden brown and crispy, about 2-3 minutes for seafood and 3-4 minutes for vegetables. Use a slotted spoon or wire mesh skimmer to transfer the tempura to a wire rack or paper towel-lined plate to drain excess oil. Sprinkle with a pinch of salt while still hot.
6. Repeat the process with the remaining ingredients, adjusting the temperature of the oil as needed to maintain a consistent frying temperature.
7. Serve the tempura hot, with tempura dipping sauce (Tentsuyu) on the side for dipping. Garnish with grated daikon radish, grated ginger, and shichimi togarashi if desired. Tempura is traditionally enjoyed with steamed rice on the side.
8. Enjoy your homemade Japanese Tempura!

Note: For a lighter and crispier tempura, it's essential to keep the batter cold and to fry the ingredients in small batches. Additionally, using high-quality, fresh ingredients will enhance the flavor of the tempura.

Thai Mango Sticky Rice

Ingredients:

For the sticky rice:

- 1 cup glutinous rice (also known as sticky rice or sweet rice)
- 1 cup coconut milk
- 1/2 cup water
- 1/4 cup sugar
- 1/2 teaspoon salt

For the coconut sauce:

- 1 cup coconut milk
- 2 tablespoons sugar
- 1/4 teaspoon salt
- 1 tablespoon cornstarch (optional, for thickening)

For serving:

- 2 ripe mangoes, peeled and sliced
- Toasted sesame seeds or mung beans (optional, for garnish)

Instructions:

1. Rinse the glutinous rice under cold water until the water runs clear. Soak the rice in water for at least 4 hours or overnight.
2. Drain the soaked rice and transfer it to a steamer lined with cheesecloth or a clean kitchen towel. Steam the rice over medium heat for 25-30 minutes, or until tender and cooked through.
3. While the rice is steaming, prepare the coconut sauce. In a small saucepan, combine the coconut milk, sugar, and salt. Bring the mixture to a gentle simmer over medium heat, stirring occasionally.

4. If you prefer a thicker sauce, mix the cornstarch with a tablespoon of water to make a slurry. Gradually add the cornstarch slurry to the coconut milk mixture, stirring constantly, until the sauce thickens slightly. Remove the saucepan from heat and set aside.
5. Once the rice is cooked, transfer it to a mixing bowl. In a separate saucepan, combine the coconut milk, water, sugar, and salt for the sticky rice. Heat the mixture over medium heat, stirring constantly, until the sugar and salt are dissolved.
6. Pour the hot coconut milk mixture over the cooked sticky rice and stir to coat the rice evenly. Let the rice sit for 10-15 minutes to absorb the coconut milk mixture.
7. To serve, divide the sticky rice among serving plates. Arrange the sliced mangoes on top or on the side of the rice.
8. Drizzle the coconut sauce over the mango sticky rice. Sprinkle with toasted sesame seeds or mung beans for garnish, if desired.
9. Serve Thai Mango Sticky Rice warm or at room temperature, and enjoy the delicious combination of sweet, creamy rice with ripe mangoes!

This Thai dessert is a delightful treat that's perfect for special occasions or anytime you're craving something sweet and tropical.